Praise for *Every Job Is a Sales Job*

"I wish I had this book when I graduated college. I wish I had this book when I started in pharma sales. I wish I had this book when I *was* in pharma sales. And I wish I had written this book!"

—JAMIE REIDY, author of *Hard Sell*

"I love this book! It turns conventional sales wisdom on its head. Gone are the days of pushy salespeople hoping you'll line their pockets by buying stuff you don't need. *Every Job Is a Sales Job* makes sales a give-and-take; a two-way street; a win-win interaction."

—CURT STEINHORST, speaker, consultant, and author of *Can I Have Your Attention?*

"This book is perfect for natural-born salespeople who haven't yet self-identified as such. Even those readers who claim to be 'allergic' to selling will soon adopt an I-can-do-this attitude after the plethora of examples and tips Dr. Cindy uses to make selling simple. Highly readable."

—DIANNA BOOHER, author of *Faster, Fewer, Better Emails* and *Communicate with Confidence*

"*Every Job Is a Sales Job* . . . for the rest of your life. Every opportunity to influence another human being is a sales job . . . for the rest of your life. This book should be

required reading at all 4,000 U.S. colleges and universities. Practical life skills!"
—MICHAEL T. BOSWORTH, speaker,
sales philosopher, and author of *What Great Salespeople Do*,
Solution Selling, and *Customer Centric Selling*

"*Every Job Is a Sales Job* is an easy-to-read, magical little book that will aid our frontline staff and management to feel comfortable with all of their customer encounters, all the while helping Cole Hardware meet our company goals. Since we specialize in being helpful, this book will definitely maximize the value of all our customer interactions. I look forward to it being published so I can distribute it to our staff. Nice job, Dr. Cindy!"
—RICK KARP, president, aka "keeper of the
karma" of Cole Hardware

"*Every Job Is a Sales Job* conveys simple truths applicable to all professions and personalities. As someone who works with a variety of start-up entrepreneurs, the principles taught in this book speak volumes for why it's not just the hungry start-up that is selling something, it's all of us on a daily basis. The progressive and thoughtful ideas shared by Dr. Cindy McGovern are truths we should all apply."
—ALEX KING, founder of Archetype Legal

"This book is not so much about new concepts but rather the stories, scenarios, and real-life examples that add up to a realistic and actionable book. Dr. Cindy is an authentic storyteller. Having known her for years, I know she has

lived these techniques and has made a successful career out of training around these key concepts: Know what you want; look for opportunities; establish trust; prepare for the ask; see it through. I have two daughters entering the business world, and I see this as required reading!"
—KATHLEEN S. ELLIS, senior vice president
of CNA International Solutions

"Everyone, everywhere, needs the wisdom that Cindy McGovern drops in her fantastic book, *Every Job Is a Sales Job*. If you have ever thought to yourself, 'I can't sell' or 'Selling feels icky,' then this book is for you, but it's also for you if you don't realize you're selling all the time, personally and professionally. Dr. Cindy lays out a step-by-step process with a focus on reciprocity that destroys the negative connotations around selling and allows you to feel good, even righteous, about what you have to offer and the value you are here to bring to others."
—MAKI MOUSSAVI, transformational coach
and author of *The High Achiever's Guide*

"As a business development professional and CEO, I know how important it is to have a plan and a process. Dr Cindy takes the reader on a journey to create their own plan and develop their own process that feels authentic to them. Regardless of what your business card or title says—you are in sales and this book shows you how to sell."
—ROBIN FARMANFARMAIAN,
professional speaker, entrepreneur, and author of
The Patient as CEO and *The Thought Leader Formula*

"Successful professionals are the ones who are accountable for their actions. In *Every Job Is a Sales Job*, Dr. Cindy makes it clear that success means taking purposeful action. That starts with making a plan. It evolves into understanding what others need from you and then making it perfectly clear what you need from them. And it ends with a lifelong relationship built on truthfulness and trust. Dr. Cindy says *Every Job Is a Sales Job* is for anyone who has a job. I'd say it's for everyone, period."

—**LINDA GALINDO**, author of *The 85% Solution*

"I am a leadership/executive coach. One of the definitions of leadership is influence. Have a vision and be able to get others to buy in and commit. Dr. Cindy's five-step process can teach you the skills. You need to bring the discipline. It will change your life if you have the courage."

—**CHRIS COFFEY**, master certified coach and practice leader (Americas) at Marshall Goldsmith Stakeholder Centered Coaching

"What a breath of fresh air! *Every Job Is a Sales Job* focuses the readers on what they want and how to get it. This is the essential road map to growing personally and professionally!"

—**MARSHALL GOLDSMITH,**
#1 *New York Times* bestselling author of *Triggers*, *MOJO*, and *What Got You Here Won't Get You There*

"*Every Job Is a Sales Job* is a blueprint for anybody who has to sell anything—whether that person is in a sales job or not. Dr. Cindy's five-step process walks you through 'selling' from making a plan all the way to making the sale. If you have a job—any job—you need to read this book. It will make you unstoppable!"

—ALDEN MILLS, an Inc. 500 CEO,
keynote speaker, CXO advisor, former Navy SEAL,
and author of *Unstoppable Teams* and *Be Unstoppable*

"Maybe you've heard it said that everybody sells, but you didn't believe it. This book will prove it true and teach you how to use it to advance your career and your organization. You won't learn gimmicks or sketchy tactics, but ethical principles of persuasion that are practical and effective. And if you already are a sales professional, this book will help make you better, too."

—MARK SANBORN, president, Sanborn &
Associates, Inc., and international bestselling author
of *The Fred Factor* and *The Intention Imperative*

"Get ready for a huge 'aha' moment that will change the way you approach every interaction you have with *Every Job Is a Sales Job*, the new book from Dr. Cindy McGovern. This empowering, actionable book first convinces you that you already have the skills to sell (it's true!) and then shares a simple road map to retrain your mind to constantly look for opportunities and get to 'yes' more often.

In Dr. Cindy's method, 'getting' is thoroughly entwined with 'giving,' resulting in long-term positive relationships without the normal 'ick factor' associated with sales. I can't recommend this book highly enough!"

—JUDY ROBINETT, business thought leader, investor, bestselling author of *Crack the Funding Code* and *How to Be a Power Connector*

"Dr. Cindy McGovern will rock your world! She transforms 'sales' from a dirty word with what she calls the 'ick' factor into the vital heartbeat of every job, through motivational coaching to psych up the reader and a systematic, practical five-step plan to demystify the sales process. Who couldn't benefit from that? If you can't hire Dr. Cindy as your sales coach, her book is the next best thing!"

—RICK BRANDON, PhD, author of the *Wall Street Journal* bestseller *Survival of the Savvy*

"*Every Job Is a Sales Job* is a goldmine for people both comfortable and uncomfortable with selling. It is not only filled with valuable tools and techniques you can immediately use, but stories that are easily relatable to drive home each point. No matter what line of work you're in, you will find this book a tremendous value as we are all selling 24/7."

—JEFF WOLF, president of Wolf Management Consultants and author of the international bestseller *Seven Disciplines of a Leader*

EVERY JOB
—— IS A ——
SALES JOB

EVERY JOB
—— IS A ——
SALES JOB

HOW TO USE THE ART

OF SELLING TO

WIN AT WORK

Dr. Cindy McGovern

New York   Chicago   San Francisco   Athens
London   Madrid   Mexico City   Milan
New Delhi   Singapore   Sydney   Toronto

1 2 3 4 5 6 7 8 9   LCR   24 23 22 21 20 19

ISBN   978-1-260-45737-7
MHID   1-260-45737-0

e-ISBN   978-1-260-45738-4
e-MHID   1-260-45738-9

This publication is designed to provide accurate and authoritative information in regard to the subject matter covered. It is sold with the understanding that neither the author nor the publisher is engaged in rendering legal, accounting, securities trading, or other professional services. If legal advice or other expert assistance is required, the services of a competent professional person should be sought.

—From a Declaration of Principles Jointly Adopted
by a Committee of the American Bar Association
and a Committee of Publishers and Associations

Library of Congress Cataloging-in-Publication Data

Names: McGovern, Cindy, author.
Title: Every job is a sales job : how to use the art of selling to win at work / by Dr. Cindy McGovern.
Description: New York : McGraw-Hill, 2020. | Description based on print version record and CIP data provided by publisher; resource not viewed.
Identifiers: LCCN 2019018832 (print) | LCCN 2019022251 (ebook) | ISBN 9781260457384 () | ISBN 1260457389 () | ISBN 9781260457377 (alk. paper) | ISBN 1260457370 (alk. paper)
Subjects: LCSH: Selling—Social aspects. | Interpersonal relations. | Success in business. | Career development.
Classification: LCC HF5438.25 (ebook) | LCC HF5438.25 .M3984 2019 (print) | DDC 658.85—dc23
LC record available at https://lccn.loc.gov/2019018832

This is for everybody who's ever said,
"But I'm not a salesperson."
I hope this book will convince you
that using the skills of the sales professional,
no matter what your job or job title,
will help make you more successful at work and at life.

Contents

CONTENTS

Introduction

I HAVE THREE IMPORTANT truths to share with you:

First, you are a salesperson. Everyone is, like it or not.

Second, you should be selling, at least unofficially, all the time.

And third, selling, even unofficially, will help your career and company.

Here's how I know that: I'm a born college professor. Or I was. Or I thought I was. I'm not anymore.

I'm a former college professor. Turns out, I'm a born salesperson.

Turns out, I'm pretty good at convincing people to do what I ask them to do. I'm persuasive, I know what I want, and I'm passionate about getting it.

That passion, when coupled with what my grandma called my "gift of gab" and my naturally outgoing nature, seems to be contagious. If I really, really believe in something, I often can infect others with that same energy and confidence. And then they want to help me. Or give something to me. Or work with me. Or be my friend.

It's a gift, I know, and I'm grateful for it, because it has helped me live my best life, both careerwise and personally.

This gift, this energy and confidence, helped me change my career path from college professor to sales consultant. It eventually led me to embrace my inner entrepreneur and open a business to help people who aren't born salespeople—and who probably don't even want to be salespeople—learn how to sell. And be more successful.

But I never, ever would have called myself a salesperson when I was a college professor. Yet, without realizing it, I sold all day long.

Guess what? So do you. No matter what you do for work. No matter if you're outgoing like me or a little shy or even an introvert.

That's an important revelation, because no matter what job you're in—college professor, lawyer, Uber driver, maintenance engineer, receptionist, coder, or anything else—you have to sell stuff. You might not think so. You might not realize it. But you do. Every day. Every single day.

As a professor, I had to sell my students on coming to class and turning in their assignments on time. As a lawyer, you have to sell clients on accepting plea deals and juries on finding your clients not guilty. As a maintenance specialist, you have to sell your company's decision makers on upgrading the equipment you need to do a good job and the people you work with on using that equipment properly. As a receptionist, you have to sell the people who walk up to your desk or call your office that you and your company are friendly and value their business. As a coder, you have to sell your colleagues or clients on approving your web page designs and taking your advice. As a manager, you have to sell your team on working together to reach a common goal.

Regardless of your job title, you have to sort of unconsciously sell people every day on believing that you're competent, deserving of their trust and future business, reliable, and nice to work with. You have to—just by the way you talk and behave—sell the customers you meet every day to believe that your company is a good one to do business with.

All day long you sell your ideas. You sell your company. You sell yourself.

Let me tell you about my own epiphany. It's the moment that led me to where I am today.

When I applied for my first nonacademic job after working as a college professor of communication for four years, I answered an ad for a consultant who would advise businesses that specialized in insurance. I had never been a consultant. And I knew nothing about insurance except how to buy it for my car.

My first interview was by phone—another first for me. During my conversation with a woman named Laura, I learned that the title of the job was actually "sales management consultant."

Oops. I had never done sales, either. Three strikes so far.

But as far as management, I knew I could do it. I also knew I was pretty good at convincing people to do stuff: the administrators at my college, my students, my friends. So I figured if I could get an in-person interview, I would be gold.

I set out on a mission: to convince Laura, over the phone, to call me in for a second interview, this time in person. I knew that if I could look her in the eye, I could convince her that I was coachable and teachable and that I could do this job. I knew that if I could meet her in person, she would see my passion.

I drew on all the communication techniques that I learned in graduate school and that I had taught my college students: I mirrored her language and her speech patterns. I exercised active listening. I made a connection with her.

I got the second interview. And guess what? I got the job.

I didn't know it at the time, but the process I used is the same one that the most successful professional salespeople use to sell stuff: They do their homework and plan for the transaction. They look for their opportunity. They establish trust with the person they're dealing with. They ask for what they want. And they follow up after they have their answer.

I didn't realize that's what I was doing. But it turns out, Laura did. She recognized my ability to sell, and she knew I could do the job. She knew something about me that I didn't know. She knew I was a salesperson. And after she hired me, she helped me embrace my inner salesperson at a time when I still believed that all sales were cheesy.

In fact, it never occurred to me until about six months later, when my boss at this same consulting firm moved me—kicking and screaming—from consultant to salesperson, that I was onto something big: I had realized that the skills I used to get into that company are the same tactics that sales professionals use every day to sell their companies' products and services to potential clients.

That was an aha moment that eventually convinced me to write this book. I had sold myself to Laura over the phone and to Laura's boss, once I met him in person. I sold him on my potential, even though I was far less than experienced in consulting and sales. I realized selling isn't something that only professional salespeople do.

It's something all professionals do.

Selling is what I've always done every time I had to convince somebody to give me what I wanted or needed. I was selling all day long, on and off the job, but I never put that label on it.

You haven't either, right? Call it what you want. It's still sales.

The biggest thunderbolt struck me when I realized that everyone is a salesperson, nearly every day, no matter what the job title is. The cashier at a sandwich shop sells customers on adding a soda and chips to their orders. The mechanic at the car dealership sells drivers on paying to have their tires rotated so they'll last longer. The civic association president sells the neighbors on spending a beautiful Saturday morning indoors at a meeting so they can vote on some new rules. The radio talk show host sells listeners on staying tuned until after the commercial break. Computer technicians at the help desk of a big-box store sell customers on buying their next electronic device at that same store by treating them and their problems as important and by never talking down to them.

It's like this phenomenon called blue car syndrome: Once you see something—or in this case, realize something—you see it everywhere. Like if you buy a blue car, then all of a sudden you notice that blue cars are everywhere.

Sorry. Didn't mean to get all college professory. I guess I'm a little bit of a nerd at heart.

——————— ———————

So we all know this now: You sell, even if it's not an official part of your job.

But how do you do this "newfound" job better than you are right now?

By working through the steps of *Every Job Is a Sales Job*.

Did I just hear you say "ick"? I know; I used to feel that way about sales, too.

But you can stop kicking and screaming! My five-step sales formula for people who are not sales professionals is in no way, shape, or form pushy, cheesy, high pressure, or unethical. It's more give-and-take. It's more like, What can I do for you, and what can you do for me?

My formula will show you how to sell in a nice way. I play nice when I sell. I always play nice. So I won't ask you to do anything but be yourself and respect the people you work with.

This five-step process will come in handy when you find yourself faced with an opportunity to sell. It's a sort of blueprint for using the skills of the sales professional to get referrals, retain clients, impress visitors, influence your boss, or otherwise sell someone on yourself and your company.

My formula will come in handy whether you're a free-lancer, contractor, teacher, or construction worker. You'll use it if you're an employee, manager, executive, or business owner.

For managers, it will help you create a culture at work that encourages nonsales employees to bring in new business and rewards them when they do.

That fact is that anyone who has a job—any job—sells, or should sell. Even those whose work titles do not include the word "sales," even those who would rather be unemployed than accept a sales job, are selling—or should be and could be—every day. If they're not, they're not doing their best work.

Every Job Is a Sales Job has two goals:

1. To convince you that everyone who works, sells, like it or not—including you.
2. To teach you how to sell successfully, even though you do not work in an official capacity as a salesperson.

This is the book that I wish someone had given me when I made the transition from college professor to consultant to sales professional early in my career.

To be honest, I wish someone had given me this book before I even accepted my first job out of college as a professor of communication. I know now that I was selling students, administrators, other faculty, and even office managers every time I needed a signature on a form, permission to attend a conference, or a better effort on an undergraduate assignment.

But I didn't realize it then. If I had, I would have done way more of it.

If I had had this book way back then, it would have saved me a lot of time "figuring it out."

THE FORMULA

Every Job Is a Sales Job is broken into two parts.

In Part 1, I reveal both obvious and hidden opportunities for employees with any job title to attract new business, to retain existing customers, and to spot opportunities to sell themselves and their ideas. I will share a secret that inevitably will lead to the aha moment when you will realize that you already sell all the time—and therefore, you already know how to sell.

In Part 2, I will break my process into five steps that show you exactly how to employ the tactics, secrets, and strategies of successful sales pros so you can use them when opportunities to "sell" yourself or your company arise.

The first step is to *plan*. Here, we will figure out what you really want and plan a way to achieve that.

The second step is to *look for opportunities* to make those sales.

The third step is to *establish trust* with the people who can help you.

The critical fourth step is to *ask for what you want.*

And finally, the fifth step is to *follow up*, no matter if the answer was yes or no, to maintain relationships—and to pay it forward.

Through these five steps and the lessons taught throughout this book, I will convince you that "getting" is indelibly intertwined with "giving." And perhaps most importantly, I will help you overcome the learned limitation of fear when it comes to asking for what you want, need, and deserve.

I will also address what I like to call the "ick" factor of sales. My guess is that you would rather do without than do anything that resembles sales. I was just like that, too, until I discovered a kinder, lighter-touch style of sales based on clarity, listening, mutual benefit, and gratitude. That is what I introduce in *Every Job Is a Sales Job*.

If you're like most people, you are reluctant to ask for what you want. You might not even believe you deserve it. So you rarely ever ask for what you want. Or for what you deserve.

The fact is that employees who ask a customer or potential client, a friend, a colleague, or anyone else to do business with a company, to buy something, or to do anything, really, are exponentially more likely to hear a "yes" than if they don't ask.

Likewise, someone who is brave enough to ask for a job or a raise is more likely to get it. There's simply no reason why you should settle for what is offered if you believe you deserve more. Whether it's a higher salary, a vacation, a great work schedule, or a job, you deserve more.

And if you don't think you deserve more, I hope to convince you that you do, in fact, deserve more. I'm going to help you overcome the fear of rejection that might be preventing you from asking for what you want, need, and deserve.

Maybe you just don't know how to ask. Or perhaps it doesn't even occur to you that you should or can ask.

By the time you finish reading *Every Job Is a Sales Job*, you will. You will know how to use proven sales strategies to come out on top during every one of the constant interactions, which are really transactions, that any employee of any company makes throughout the day. *Every Job Is a Sales Job* will lay out a formula for turning that "Nice doing business with you" handshake into a request for future business in a way that is fair to both giver and receiver and that is comfortable even for those who are shy or lack confidence.

And it will fire you up to do that without resorting to the cheesy, pushy tactics so often associated with used car sales or time-shares. But frankly, even those salespeople are moving away from those tactics.

This brings to mind the signs I used to see at every restaurant, gas station, and store that said, "Come again." We should do that every time we meet with people: Invite them to come back.

Don't assume that your excellent service speaks for itself and that your client or customer will automatically come back for more. Instead, come right out and ask for what you want.

EVERY JOB

— IS A —

SALES JOB

I DIDN'T EXPECT THIS

CHAPTER 1

So You're Not in Sales?

A FEW YEARS BACK, I was living in Washington, D.C. The first 95-degree day that summer was also the first day of the season that broke 80 degrees. We'd had a long winter and an unseasonably cool spring, so even by mid-June I had never cranked up the air conditioning in the row house where I was living with my husband.

When I did flip the thermostat on to turn on the air conditioning for the first time on that sweltering day, nothing happened.

By the time a few hours had gone by, the house was unbearably hot. I called for help.

The technician who came over was friendly and courteous. He covered his dusty work boots with what my grandma used to call "footies"—the footwear equivalent of a shower cap—so he wouldn't track dirt onto my clean carpet. He made polite conversation with me. He listened carefully as I described the problem I was having with the AC. He checked out the thermostat, asked where he could find the outdoor condenser, and crawled into the attic to examine the ductwork. He explained the problem to me, gave me a couple of options, with prices, and asked if I had any questions.

I'm a chatty person, so along the way I told him that my gas furnace had leaked all winter, but thankfully had never shut down. I said I guessed it just wasn't my year for smooth sailing with appliances.

We agreed that he would replace the air conditioner's motor the following week. Then he asked me something I didn't expect: Could he see my gas furnace?

I took him to the utility closet and showed him the water stain on the floor.

He gave the unit a careful once-over and told me why the furnace had leaked and what he could do to solve the problem. We agreed that he would do that repair the following week, too.

He left my home with two pricey jobs to complete the next week. Why? He saw an opportunity to sell me a furnace repair while the actual job was just to service my air conditioner.

The tech—Ben—isn't a salesperson. He's a highly skilled HVAC technician. He doesn't get a commission for adding a furnace job onto an AC service call. He isn't responsible for bringing extra business into the company. Nobody told him he should look at the furnace. It was summertime, and he was there to solve an air-conditioning problem, period.

But he sold me nonetheless.

Ben probably wouldn't even call that a sale. He'd call it a common courtesy. Or maybe a chance to help a customer out. Or just doing a good job. He's just a nice guy who heard me say I had a problem, and he knew how to solve it. So he offered and I accepted.

Call it what you want, but I call that a sale.

The company wins. Ben wins. I win.

Just because your job title doesn't include the word "sales" doesn't mean you can't or shouldn't sell.

My advice: You should sell. And sell as often as possible.

Selling is everybody's job. Without sales, none of us would have a job to come to tomorrow.

WHO SHOULD SELL?

Everyone who meets other people as part of his or her routine duties is in the perfect position to sell additional products and services to those people. They could be customers or clients. They could be visitors to the company headquarters. They could be the neighbors or friends you talk to about work after hours.

I can almost hear you saying, "But sales is not my job." Isn't it though?

Whether you're the president of the company or a member of the cleaning crew, if you come into contact with people—the public, your colleagues, or anyone, really—during your workday, you have a chance to sell.

If you're well dressed, pleasant to be around, good at making small talk, and interested in hearing what people have to say, you can sell. If you're quiet but you're a good listener—even if you're shy—you can sell.

If you have a skill that you can use to solve problems for other people, you can sell.

In fact, you already do. Every time you make a good impression on anybody you meet in conjunction with your job, that person becomes more likely to use your company again the next time he or she needs a product or a service like the one your company specializes in. That's a potential sale.

I knew before Ben ever left my house that day that I was going to call his company again next time I needed an HVAC tech. In fact, I knew Ben would be my "guy" every time. I would request him.

He made a sale that neither he nor I expected when he first walked through my front door. He also made a customer for life. He made such a good impression that I told all my neighbors about him, and some of them called his company.

That's going to add up to lots of extra sales over the years.

Chances are good that you have made this kind of unexpected sale, too—or that you could have if you had paid closer attention to what your customer was telling you.

For example, whenever you run into a mom at your kid's ball game who asks you where you work, she becomes more likely to call you if she needs something your company offers—if you've talked about work in a positive way. That's a potential sale.

Of course, the opposite is true as well. If you bad-mouth your company after hours, you could give people a bad impression of your workplace. That's the opposite of a sale.

So whenever you meet an old school pal for lunch, talk enthusiastically about the project you're working on or an opportunity your boss just offered you. That way you plant the seed that your employer is a good one. Your pal might someday recommend you or your company, or apply for a job there himself.

That's a sale.

Whenever you work with a client or a customer and you get an inkling that the person isn't too happy with another company she's using for a service that your firm offers, too, you have the opportunity to bring that business on board. Do it, and you've made a sale.

PRO TIP

In sales lingo, that's called "qualifying" a client. The simple act of introducing these qualified clients to the real sales pros in your company is as good as bringing money into the business.

What kinds of skills do you use when you want to convince the board of directors to approve a new education program for stakeholders? Or wow a client into choosing your creative idea for an ad campaign instead of someone else's? Or get buy-in from your staff when you decide to add Saturday shifts to their traditional weekday-only schedules?

Sales skills.

None of those tasks is an add-on; none of them is something you would turn over to a sales professional instead of doing it yourself. Yet you're using the skills of the sales pro every time you make a pitch, a request, or a change that involves other people.

You sell, sell, sell all day.

But you don't call it sales. You just call it "doing your job."

SHIFT THE WAY YOU THINK

Now that you understand that you have the potential to sell in unexpected ways, it's time to shift the way you think so you can easily identify sales opportunities going forward.

Think about what you have sold at work today, and to whom. Did you get a colleague to cover your phone for you so you could take an extra half hour at lunchtime for a physical therapy appointment? Did you convince a caller to hold for an extended time so you could figure out how to fill her unusual request? Did you ask the coworker who sits in the next cubicle to turn the volume down on the music he streams on his computer all day? Did you collect a past-due payment from a client whose account has been delinquent for six months?

How did you do that?

You used the skills of the sales professional. You sold them on it.

You didn't even realize you were selling, but you were.

A client of mine, Martin, was an insurance under-writer for years and years before his boss promoted him into the position of sales manager. Martin came to me for advice because my work involves helping nonsalespeople excel at sales.

"I'm not a salesperson," Martin kept telling me. Even after he became the sales manager, he insisted that he was in management, not sales.

It wasn't too long before the sales team he managed outsold every competitor in his market. Martin still refused to call himself a salesperson.

I hoped to convince him to embrace his inner sales professional. I asked him why he thought his boss pro-moted him into this job.

"I've been with the company a long time," he replied.

My response: "Nope, it's because you sold him on it. You sold him on your ability to manage a sales force even though you're not a trained sales professional."

I told him: "You can tell me all day that you're not a salesperson. But you went from a middle manager to the hiring manager to the sales manager. You got there by selling yourself to the higher-ups."

It took some doing, but I finally convinced Martin that he has been selling every day since he joined the company 10 years ago. He just never realized that's what he was doing.

Imagine if he had. Imagine if he had been selling on purpose instead of doing it without realizing it. Imagine how much more successful he might be by now.

Martin's passion is helping people. Now that he realizes that he excels as a salesperson, he can help so many more people.

Embrace your inner salesperson. Know that your job is sales, even if it's not your title on your business card. Consider every interaction a transaction, and every transaction a sale.

In the chapters that follow, I'm going to teach you how to do this without resorting to the "ick" tactics of unscrupulous sales reps. I'm going to remind you that you already do this every day.

CHAPTER 2

You Know More Than You Think

Have you ever convinced:

- A six-year-old to eat broccoli (or anything green)?
- A neighbor to feed your cat while you're away on vacation?
- A coworker to swap shifts with you so you could have the day off?
- A teacher to accept a late assignment?

Have you ever gotten:

- The job you applied for after having a good interview?
- The raise that you asked for?
- A second chance with a client or colleague after messing up your first encounter?
- A referral from a client or from a colleague at another company?

Nice work! In all of these situations, you made the sale.

The fact is that every transaction that could result in a "yes" or a "no" will require you to sell something: yourself, your idea, a concept, your worthiness, your value, your competence, your company.

And you've done it countless times. You do it dozens of times every day, on and off the job. You're good at it. You just didn't realize it.

Remember the example I mentioned in the Introduction, when I convinced a sales consulting company specializing in insurance to hire me even though I knew nothing about sales, consulting, or insurance? Just like me, you have sold your way into jobs, new business, awards, raises, praise, discounts, and tons of opportunities.

So don't tell me you don't know how to sell. You do it all the time.

After reading the previous chapter, you may be starting to embrace your inner salesperson. Now I want to assure you of something: You've got this!

However, now that we're putting a label on what you've been doing all along—and calling it sales—don't freak out!

You already have the important communication skills that you need to make yourself an unofficial salesperson when workplace situations arise that call for the use of sales skills.

But the funny thing is, as you become more aware of the power of the sale, you might also become more reluctant to sell.

I have a good friend, Karina, who is a writing professor. Karina tells a story about an adult student who, as she
loves to say, "couldn't write her way out of a paper bag."

Her words, not mine.

The student wrote awkward sentences full of gram-
matical errors. She placed words out of order so that the
sentences often made no sense. Her writing made her
appear uneducated, to the point that Karina wondered
how the student had ever passed a college admissions test
or gotten through her high school English courses.

It turns out that Karina wasn't half as frustrated as the
student was.

The freshman asked Karina for a private meeting to
discuss her performance in class. Karina was prepared
to offer tutoring, makeup assignments, and extra-credit
work to give the student more practice and help her writing improve.

She wasn't prepared for what happened.

The student spoke to her using perfect grammar, excellent sentence structure, clear vocabulary, and thoughtful
points.

Karina couldn't believe this was the same writer who
was stuck in that paper bag.

If she would just write the way she spoke, she would
earn As on every assignment, Karina told the student. She
asked her, "Why don't you do that?"

It seems that the student intuitively knew how to
express herself. But once she had to learn what the parts of

speech were called, that the sentence had to be ordered as "subject-verb-object," that she had to adhere to a specific word count, that she couldn't include certain details in the first paragraph, and on and on—she began to believe she didn't know how to write at all.

As the student tried to conform to the rules and not break any, she threw her intuition out the window. The rules and labels paralyzed her to the point that she simply couldn't write a coherent sentence.

She was so afraid she would do it wrong that she could barely do it at all.

The same thing happens when it comes to knowing how to sell.

The fact is, most of us intuitively know how to get what we want—or at least we know how to try—from a very young age. Kids "work" their parents all the time to get toys, phones, clothes, and cool trips. They blatantly ask for what they want. They figure out how to butter people up and how to play mom off of dad.

Once upon a time, you knew how to do all of that, too. But somewhere along the way, someone told you to stop. Someone told you that you "can't" be so bold as to ask for what you want or that you "shouldn't" impose on someone by suggesting a favor. Or someone simply told you "no." So you got timid, shy, or careful, and you stopped asking altogether.

Around the same time, you probably started settling. Settling for what was offered instead of asking for what you deserved. Settling for something instead of everything.

Now you're reluctant to ask for a raise. You're too modest to toot your own horn in order to get that promotion. You're afraid the client will say "no" if you ask for more business, so you simply don't ask. You've dealt with enough sales professionals to know that you don't want to make someone feel as uncomfortable as you do when you buy a car or face a hard sell from one of those kiosk workers at the mall.

So now you don't dare ask. But if you don't ask, chances are good that you won't get.

But don't you want to get what you want? Don't you want what you deserve? Don't you want what you know would make you happy, successful, or proud of yourself?

You should. And the good news: That kid is still in you someplace. My hope is that I can help you recover the boldness that helped you sell so effortlessly as you did before people started telling you not to.

The fact is, nonsalespeople who don't realize that they're selling often sell up a storm. Once they realize what they're doing, though, they freak out.

The thought of selling freaks a lot of people out.

Face it: Unless you majored in marketing in college or attended a bunch of sales seminars as part of your job training, you probably never learned how to sell.

That doesn't mean you don't know how to sell; you do. It just means you don't know how to sell according to a formula or best practices or a specific process—yet.

It's a little like someone who's a really good singer but has never had voice lessons. She still knows how to sing.

15

Just because nobody calls her a musician doesn't mean she can't sing like an angel.

Does having this new knowledge make you behave differently? Does it make you afraid to try to sell—as you always have intuitively done—because you're now afraid you'll do it wrong? Or hear a "no"? Or offend someone?

OK, take a deep breath. Keep doing what you've been doing. Just do more of it. Do it on purpose. And do it with intention.

Channel your inner child—the bold one who was a born salesperson. The one who was not afraid to ask for what you wanted.

——————— ———————

Using the skills of the sales professional to get what you want and need and deserve every day—on and off the job—makes it so much more likely that you will succeed at getting those things.

Here are some of the sales tactics you may be using at work without realizing that's what they are. Have you:

- Made such a good impression on someone that he or she recommended you or your company to a colleague or a friend?
- Noticed how well you work with a particular colleague who works outside your company—and asked if you could do business together again?
- Handed your business card to someone you think might benefit from something your business offers and invited the person to call for more information?

- Invited a new acquaintance to lunch or for coffee with the hope that you can collaborate on a project?
- Come up with an argument for why you deserve a raise or promotion—based on how your success could benefit the company?
- Come right out and asked someone to do business with you or your firm?
- Requested that someone refer you or your business to his or her friends and colleagues?
- Posted on social media about your professional milestones, a project or article that you completed, or a proud moment for you or your company?
- Reached beyond the scope of a meeting or an assignment to do something extra because you realized that the client or customer needed more from you than what was originally assigned?
- Kept in touch with a client whose business with you was finished?

You're already selling, just by doing a good job. Now that you realize it, you can start selling on purpose.

PRO TIP

If you're a manager, you can use this process to create a culture at work that encourages nonsales employees to bring in new business and rewards them when they do.

CHAPTER 3

Hey, By the Way

IF YOU'VE EVER BOUGHT a house or a condo, you might have noticed that your real estate agent isn't the only one at the settlement table who is selling.

When it's time to sign on the dotted line, you sit at a big conference table with a bunch of people, like a real estate agent, a lawyer, a closing agent from a title company, and maybe even a loan officer. The homeowners who are selling you the house might be there, too.

The real estate agent probably knows everyone at the table, but the rest of you very likely are meeting face-to-face for the first time.

Let's say this settlement meeting goes well. Everyone signs lots of papers; there are no surprises or delays. The meeting ends with handshakes all around and even a couple of hugs, and a selfie for social media. Everyone leaves happy.

But they skipped a step.

Everyone at that meeting left some important, unfinished business on the table. Each missed an obvious opportunity to ask for future business from all the others.

Why not ask the others if they would like to work together on the next closing? Why not ask each other for referrals to future clients? Why not ask the buyers and sellers if they would be willing to refer the people at the table to their friends and to keep them in mind when they're ready to buy or sell again? Why not set up a meeting with one or all of these new colleagues to talk about working together some more?

Every settlement needs some combination of a lawyer, a lender, a title expert, and a Realtor. Why not use this golden opportunity to land some more business for each of their firms?

Here's why not: It probably didn't occur to any of them—except, perhaps, the real estate agent. The agent is a professional salesperson, and the rest are not.

Or are they?

Yes, they are. Everyone at that table has a sales job. Every job is a sales job, no matter what your job title says.

These sales where you don't "officially" have to sell, but you see an opportunity to sell, are what I call "Hey, by the way" sales.

My air-conditioning guy, Ben, is a master of the "Hey, by the way" sale. As I described it earlier, he listens carefully to the homeowners he meets, and so he hears them when they mention a problem, often in an offhand way, that isn't part of his job assignment for the day. He offers to help with the second problem—help that his company will bill the customer for.

Before he leaves someone's house, he asks, "Is there anything else I can do for you before I go?"

A flip-side story: Angelo is one of the most talented home improvement pros I've ever met. Unfortunately, he is just the opposite of Ben. He leaves opportunities for sales on the table, along with the money they could make for his company, all the time.

Like the waitress in a restaurant who says, "This isn't my table" when you ask for a clean fork, Angelo refuses to add any new tasks onto an existing contract if they weren't agreed to before he started the work.

For example, he was building a patio for a couple I know, and they really loved his work. As he dug ditches and laid pavers and added a retaining wall in the backyard, the wife asked him if he would be willing to replace the rusty railing on the back porch before he finished up.

He said "no." That wasn't part of the job they agreed to. He complained that customers were always trying to get him to add onto jobs. He implied that she was trying to get him to do extra work for free, but she wasn't. She knew she would have to pay more for labor and materials, and she was willing to do so.

What I think Ben would have said is, "Sure, that will only cost you an extra $200," or whatever the price is. He would have made that sale—and many others. Instead, Angelo walked away from that money, and he left a bad impression on the wife, who was in a position to recommend him to her neighbors.

But she never did because he just said "no."

The key to any sale, as you'll learn in Part 2, is listening. The key to good listening is hearing people's problems and requests without making assumptions. A good unofficial salesperson, or even a pro, for that matter, responds to those requests with potential solutions and information—like how much the solution will cost.

Why leave $200 on the table, especially when you weren't even expecting to earn it? Not every sale is the result of a formal, planned request. Especially for people who do not sell in an official capacity, some sales can seem like they've come out of nowhere—as if they've dropped out of the sky and into your lap.

You can catch what falls into your lap, or you can stand up, brush it off, and walk away. I'm guessing that like most people, you're smart enough to know that if you act on these unexpected opportunities, you will help yourself or your company succeed.

Your boss will like it if you are—or can become—one of those people.

Sales opportunities can appear any time: during a casual conversation, after you meet someone new, or while working on one project and not even thinking about the next.

Sales opportunities very often come out of the blue, and they happen naturally.

Train yourself to listen for them. Train yourself to follow up with questions. Train yourself to quickly respond with potential solutions and information.

A dermatologist who was conducting a routine skin check on my friend Angelique did just that.

During the visit, Angelique asked the doctor if there was any way to get rid of a cluster of sun spots on the side of her face. The doctor told her about cryotherapy—a process a dermatologist can use to freeze spots off skin—and offered to do it right then. Angelique wound up identifying about a dozen spots on her body that she wanted removed, and the dermatologist happily complied.

This isn't an insurance-related procedure, so Angelique paid for it herself—and was happy to. She had asked another dermatologist about sun spots a year earlier and had simply been told, "I don't offer any treatment for sun spots."

Angelique's current dermatologist made a "Hey, by the way" sale to a patient who will tell her friends.

Sarah, another acquaintance of mine, works in public relations and was assigned to write a brochure and shoot a promotional video for a new pet spa. The owners, a young couple, had been getting a lot of requests for information and media interviews since they opened the store, the first one in their county.

The couple had decided that the wife would be the spokesperson for the store and meet with reporters who requested interviews. But during Sarah's promotional shoot, she realized that the woman was extremely camera-shy.

"Hey, by the way," Sarah offered, "I can teach you how to overcome that. I can give you some training on how to look and act on camera and on what you should say to reporters."

Sarah's assignment was to get in and get out and move onto the next job. This was a one-time deal. But she offered the extra service, which, of course, came with an upcharge from Sarah's company, and the woman agreed.

The pet spa became a recurring client of Sarah's PR firm rather than a one-and-done job.

Before that meeting, Sarah thought she was just a writer and photographer. After, she proved to be a salesperson and a consultant, too!

Like all of us should and can do, Sarah sells when the opportunity arises. She sells without thinking, "Hey, I can make a sale here." In fact, she wasn't thinking about making money for her company when she offered to help this client; she just saw that she could solve a problem that the woman clearly needed help solving. She saw that she could help her client and did what professional salespeople call "consultative sales."

–––––––– ––––––––

"Hey, by the way" sales often are simply a reaction to a circumstance. The dermatologist didn't know Angelique would be asking her about sun spots during her skin check. Sarah never suspected the woman at the pet spa would need media coaching.

PRO TIP

Consultative sales is a way to sell that uncovers the needs of the other person. It's about helping others by offering them solutions to their needs.

The fact is, selling doesn't always involve money or merchandise.

What do you have—or what does your business do—that could potentially solve a problem for someone else?

But when it came to their attention, they responded. They listened, they heard, and they offered a potential solution. They made the sale.

Train yourself to recognize opportunities when they present themselves. Know that they present themselves every single day. Make yourself comfortable with asking for what you want, on the fly.

In short, put yourself in a frame of mind to ask for what you want or can offer whenever the opportunity arises. Consciously look for opportunities, and you'll never overlook them.

You also can create opportunities for "Hey, by the way" sales. You actually can plan to make "accidental" sales by putting yourself in situations where those opportunities might arise.

Some examples:

- **If you make speeches for work, offer to answer questions, one-on-one, with audience members after your presentation.** Experts who make speeches often are invited to speak elsewhere, to consult on projects, and to write articles.
- **Accept invitations to networking events.** Socializing with colleagues can help you get to know what your coworkers need. Offer solutions to those problems—and you'll find that they might be able to help you get what you need, as well. Mingling with professionals who work in the same field as you—but in other organizations—gives you the same opportunity to offer your company's services to potential new clients.
- **Volunteer in your community.** Not only is this the perfect way to give back, but it's a natural way to introduce yourself, your services, and your organization to people through casual conversations.
- **Talk about work when you sit with other parents at your kids' ball games and school functions.** You never know when someone might ask you for your professional advice about something—and wind up asking for an introduction to someone at your firm.
- **Tell people what you do at work.** Whoever it is—friends, acquaintances, the person behind you in line at Starbucks—tell them. You or your business might have just the expertise someone is looking for—but didn't know how to find.

- **Before you finish any conversation about work, ask if the other person would be willing to refer you and your company to colleagues and friends.** Most people are, indeed, willing to do that, but it won't occur to them unless you ask for it.
- **As you finish one job, ask for your next one.** "Hey, by the way," you might say, "I have some free time next month. Could you use some help again next month?"
- **Ask others to share their contacts with you.** My neighbor told me about a great housekeeper she found through a friend. The first time the house-keeper worked at my neighbor's house, she asked, "Do you have any neighbors who might be looking for a cleaning service?" My friend said she did, and the housekeeper asked her for their names and e-mail addresses so she could contact them.
- **Make a list of what you need.** Whether it's an introduction to the CEO of the company you want to work for next, the e-mail address of an author you would like to speak to your staff, or a copy of a report that's not going to be released to the public until next week—keep a list of what you want. You never know when it will come in handy.

If you know what you want and keep it top of mind, you'll be able to ask for it if a "Hey, by the way" moment presents itself to you.

PART 2

DR. CINDY'S FIVE STEPS FOR MAKING A SALE

CHAPTER 4

—— STEP ONE ——

Plan

THE FIRST AND MOST critical part of my five-step process for unofficial selling is planning.

I'm going to answer your question before you ask it: Why would you spend time planning to do something that you're not expected to do, or paid to do, or trained to do? Or maybe you don't even want to do it?

Because every job is a sales job, even yours.

You make sales every day, even if you don't call them that. You negotiate; you convince; you talk people into stuff; you ask for favors; you pitch ideas. It's so natural, so much a part of your day, that you do it without realizing it. Sometimes you might even do it by accident. It happens if it happens.

You do it without a plan, and you're pretty good at it.

Imagine how much better you would be at it if you had a plan for it.

How much more would you sell if you planned ahead? How many more opportunities would come your way if you planned to keep your eyes and ears open for opportunities to boost your company's reputation or your own? How much better prepared would you be if you planned exactly how you would ask for the job, or the raise, or the project, so you knew exactly what to say if the opportunity happened to fall into your lap?

You will be more successful at work if you plan ahead, just in case the opportunity arises for you to ask for something you really want. Even if your nonsales selling routine involves sealing the deal over casual, impromptu opportunities, there's really nothing impromptu about successful selling.

Even if you already are super-successful at work, you will be more successful with a plan.

Planning is something we all do on some level just to stay organized. We make to-do lists. We keep calendars. We make reservations. We schedule meetings and trips. We pencil in lunch dates. We figure out how to find the time to get our work done every day.

None of that happens by accident. Even if you don't write down a formal plan every day or every week, you keep a schedule and a to-do list in your head. If you don't, you probably don't get much done every day.

Planning, in my experience, is the key to success. It's the key to getting things done. It's the key to getting started and getting finished so we can be and feel productive.

And planning is the key to making a sale.

If you're successful at your job, it's likely because you make plans. You take the steps you need to wake up in the morning (set your alarm), get to work on time (leave the house by 8 a.m.), bang out the report that's due (close your office door), eat a healthy lunch (pack it the night before), and pick up the kids from daycare (gas up the car in advance).

People who are chronically late, constantly miss their deadlines, forget appointments, overbook their schedules, or wind up working half the night on a regular basis are people who struggle with planning.

Before every day begins, I know what I will do that day—all the way to what time I'll go to sleep.

People who plan tend to sleep better. They rarely wake up in the middle of the night worrying that they forgot to do something. Or that they're going to miss a deadline. Or that they have no idea what they're going to say the next day during a client presentation. Or that they're going to be in trouble with a vendor because they forgot to send a payment.

That's what I strive for. I try to keep it all organized, written down, and scheduled.

Yes, I'm that girl.

Planning helps me get more done. It keeps me on track. It allows me to finish every day without leaving anything undone. It gives me the chance to have a great home life and social life. It helps me earn more money. It helps me feel like I am running my day, instead of letting my day run me.

Planning does take time, though. But it's one of the most important parts of success in selling.

Even though I'm a consultant, I still sell, sell, sell every day. So I plan for that. In fact, my business card says "First Lady of Sales."

I sell when I meet a potential new client and explain how the services my company offers can solve a problem for his company.

I sell when I coach that client's employees about strategies for selling more successfully. I have to convince them not only to buy into my five-step sales process, but to actually get out there and try it.

I sell when I call a client and recommend that she keep me on the clock for a few more hours that week so I can spend extra time with one of her employees who is struggling with his sales quotas.

I sell when I have to work overtime and I ask my assistant to stay an extra two hours to help me.

I know I have to sell not only to keep my business afloat by bringing in new clients, but to keep myself on track so I can take good care of each client and devote plenty of time to each one.

You think I'd leave any of that up to chance? Or luck? Or happenstance?

Nope.

Because I realize that I am a salesperson for my company, I prepare myself for the sales that I will make every day. I'm even prepared for the ones I don't know I will make—the ones that spring from unexpected opportunities while I'm doing something else.

I would sell so much less if I did not have my plan. You will sell so much more once you have yours.

———————   ———————

I've divided the rest of this chapter into three sections to help you embrace your role as an unofficial salesperson for your business.

First, I'll share with you the importance of selling in a way that feels authentic, ethical, and natural for you.

Second, I'll offer some advice about the value of planning, both for long-term goals and for today's sales.

Third, I'll discuss why it's so important for managers and business owners—no matter what industry or trade you work in—to create a sales culture at work that encourages all employees to bring in new business and that rewards them for doing so.

This is not the only place in the book where you will read about planning. It's so important to every person who works anywhere that I incorporate it into every step and every chapter.

If you can make a plan, you can make a sale. Let's start with the plan.

AUTHENTIC

Nobody likes to be sold, but everybody likes to buy. It's all around us.

In fact, people who have not chosen sales as a profession rarely like doing the selling.

The good news is that sellers and buyers work well together because a casual sale can truly be a casual experience for both of you.

Selling shouldn't make you feel cheesy or the person you're selling feel used or conned. It shouldn't even feel like selling at all. It shouldn't feel like being sold at all.

In fact, a sale is simply a transaction that occurs during an interaction between two people. It's not much different from arranging to have lunch with a colleague: You negotiate the time, the place, and the restaurant. You decide whether to invite others. You determine whether you can expense the meal or who will pick up the tab. You agree about how much time you both can take out of your busy day. You record the date on your calendar. You touch base the morning of. You arrange where you will meet and whether you will walk or Uber to the restaurant.

In short, you're trying to make a sale. You want to go at noon to the Mexican place down the block tomorrow because you're scouting venues for a big employee retirement reception. Expensing the meal seems reasonable, given that you'll be on a scouting trip. You only have an hour and a half free for lunch. You'd like to walk there and back to get some fresh air and exercise. You'll send a quick text to your colleague in the morning and suggest that you meet in the office lobby.

The negotiation results in a scenario similar to that, but with a few accommodations to your friend, who only has an hour and can't leave the office until 12:15.

Sale.

Wait. Sale?

Yes. That's a sale. You both wanted something from the other. You had to do a little give-and-take, but you both got what you wanted.

It was fair, flexible, casual, and successful.

You do this every day.

Do it more often. Do it on behalf of your company. Do it for yourself.

Plan to do it.

Say the two of you walk over to that Mexican restaurant, and you notice that the bar would be the perfect place to host the party, if the owner would be willing to shut it down for a couple of hours on a weeknight later in the month.

After lunch, you and your colleague approach the manager and ask if that's possible. He says he'll check with the owner. You exchange business cards.

Before the owner calls, you do some planning. You check with accounting and learn that your budget for the party is $2,000, including the room and refreshments. You ask the soon-to-be retiree if she likes Mexican food. You make sure your own schedule is clear.

The owner calls later. He says he's willing to shut the bar down if you're willing to guarantee that your party will spend at least $2,000 on drinks in those two hours.

You say that might be too steep for just cocktails, and you ask if the tally could include the purchase of appetizers like chips and salsa and mini quesadillas.

You work out the date and time. The owner says "yes." You say "yes." He gets business on a slow Tuesday evening. You get a nice venue for the reception.

Sale.

That's not intimidating, is it? So why does the idea of making other types of sales feel so scary?

Booking a restaurant for a work party isn't any different from asking people to refer their friends and colleagues to your business. It isn't any different from telling a client who is already working with you that your company has another service that might help her and then asking if she'd like to hear about it. It isn't any different from mentioning a charity book auction your firm is hosting to someone you just met in line at Starbucks who has just told you he likes old books.

So many people believe that making a sale means pressuring someone into buying something he or she doesn't want or need, or can't afford.

I don't do that, and I sell all the time. I don't want you to do that, either. Ever.

To me, making a sale means offering something that you believe might be of interest or value or use to someone else. Making a sale means politely requesting that someone buy from or trade with or give something to you in exchange for something as simple as a "thank you" or a warm feeling or a favor in return.

I sell on my own terms. I never push or pressure or bait or ridicule or lie or force.

That's just not me. That's not my style, and it goes against what I think is ethical and fair.

Instead, I listen and observe to learn if the other person might need or want something I have to offer. I tell what I know about the product or service. If I'm making a request—like asking for a referral—I explain why I believe I deserve it and that I will thank the person by doing a good job if his friends and colleagues hire me. I directly ask the person for what I want.

But before I do any of that, I plan for the transaction.

I study my own steps: Step One, of course, is planning. Step Two is looking for opportunities. Step Three is establishing trust, truly listening, and sizing up the situation. Step Four is asking for what I want. Step Five is following up.

I study them so I don't forget to do them. It's easy, in the moment, to get flustered if things don't go exactly as you thought they would.

With a plan, you can stay on track, no matter what.

It's easy to get tongue-tied when an unexpected opportunity finds you.

With a plan, you will have given a lot of thought to what you would say if that ever happened.

It's easy to chicken out when it's time to ask for the sale, the favor, the referral, or the promotion.

With a plan, you will have rehearsed this moment a dozen times.

It's easy to feel mortified if the answer is "no" when you hoped for and expected a "yes."

With a plan, you will have already braced yourself to be gracious and grateful no matter what the answer. You will have a plan for the answer, whatever it is.

A plan can go a long way toward taking the fear out of any transaction. A plan helps you be yourself during the transaction.

It's always a risk when you ask someone for something and you're not sure if the answer will be "yes" or "no." You risk feeling rejected if the answer is "no."

A plan makes the "ask" way less risky.

It also helps ensure that you will be you while you're making your sale.

My client Anna is a sales rep for a big company in Texas. She has a genuine passion for helping people. She likes sales because she knows that she helps a lot of people out by putting them together with services and products that will solve their problems and make their jobs easier.

But she felt bad about selling. She bought into the notion that salespeople are sleazy and dishonest. She felt beaten down by acquaintances and even friends and family who constantly berated her for being in a profession known for its high-pressure tactics and disregard for the well-being of others.

Because of this, she told me, she felt she was "beneath" the people she was selling to. She felt like she had to grovel for their business. She didn't believe she deserved the "yes" she was asking for.

So she did things to sweeten every deal, like offering free tickets to sporting events. But doing that made her feel even worse. She felt like she was bribing people to do business with her.

I suggested that she try my five-step approach for a month. I encouraged her to recognize the value that she delivers to her clients and to realize that she does deserve to be successful in her sales job. I urged her to change her mentality about salespeople.

I reminded her that so few salespeople actually fit into that clichéd mold. I assured her she was not one of them.

I coached her to be herself. To act as if she were talking to people she already knew and cared about. To sell them only what they needed and wanted. To stop trying to buy their business with basketball tickets.

Her first step was to make a plan. I asked her to identify what she really wanted to do with her life and career. She came back to what she always says, because it's genuine: "I want to help people."

I asked her to consider whether sales is a way for her to help people. So she examined the services she was selling and came to a conclusion: yes.

Then I guided her to evaluate whether the way she was selling was a reflection of her values and character. This time the answer was no.

She got to work planning a change. She would stop groveling for business. She would stop emulating salespeople who did that. She would alter her approach so it suited her personality. She would start treating sales as a service rather than as a job. The change in her was almost immediate.

Anna is a straight shooter. She actually told me, "I don't feel like I have to go in and pimp myself out anymore to get deals."

Now, she said, "I feel like I'm really helping people. I see myself as their equal."

She seems to realize that she deserves to be happy and successful. She realizes she is offering a useful service that people need and want.

And she has a plan that she reviews before every sales call. It's a plan that outlines how she will approach people, which questions she will ask them, what she will offer them, how she will ask for their business, and how she will determine whether what she is selling will truly help those she hopes will buy from her.

In short, Anna couldn't be herself on sales calls before she sat down and planned how to do it. It seems counterintuitive, doesn't it? But a plan helped her become more authentic with her clients—and more successful.

BIG QUESTIONS

You might think you don't have time to make a plan for every sale. But the plan will help you get focused. The plan will help you stay on course and keep your goals top of mind.

Planning gives you a chance to discover what you need to be successful, whether it's over a lifetime or just on the day you're going to ask your plumber to hire your accounting firm to do his books.

Here are five important questions to answer as you make your plans:

1. What do you want?

You can't make a plan until you know what your goal is.

You are extremely unlikely to get what you want if you don't know what you want. Planning gives you the opportunity to figure that out. Be honest with yourself.

Knowing what you want will help you determine what you have to do to get it. It will help you identify the people who can help you get it. It will lead you to take the action you need to take to get it.

Plans can be big or small. But they always start at the end: What's your goal? What's your endgame? Where do you want to be? Where do you want to go next?

A big plan will help you chart a course for your career. Say you're a lawyer and you want to eventually be a partner in a corporate law firm. Your plan will help you know when it's time to make each "sale" that will move you closer to the C-suite. It will be a blueprint for when to change jobs, when to throw your hat into the ring, how to approach the subject with the decision makers at your firm, and when to move to another firm if the one you work for isn't doing its part to help you reach your goals.

A small, task-specific plan, on the other hand, will prepare you for the sale you want to make right now: asking for a job or a raise; finding someone to swap shifts with you; convincing your team to work this weekend; motivating your staff to work more efficiently.

My friend Carla is the public relations director for a large professional development company that companies hire when their employees need to learn about job-related technology. Part of her job is to get media coverage for the company's new courses.

The director of the department responsible for creating courses involving the most cutting-edge technology was planning to introduce a class for real estate agents, architects, journalists, and other professionals who wanted to become drone pilots.

The director told Carla all about the course. He was excited about it because no other training company in the area had anything like it. He wanted to introduce it to the company's employees and clients with a lot of fanfare at a "launch" party—pun intended—so he filled Carla in so she could start getting the publicity materials ready.

Carla was excited about the program, too. She told her staff all about it and enlisted their help to prepare press releases, news articles, and social media posts to publish to coincide with the launch party.

A couple of weeks ahead of time, Carla and her staff did a publicity blitz to create some buzz about the party and the new course. They were proud of their effort.

But the director was livid. He didn't want any publicity materials to go out until after the party. He wanted to announce the course himself at the party and surprise everyone. He felt the pre-party publicity stole his thunder.

Carla was perplexed. The director had, after all, asked her to create publicity materials—but he didn't tell her to hold off until after the party. Carla had assumed that getting people to a party generally is best accomplished if you let people know about the party before it happens.

Still, she apologized for the misunderstanding—and it truly was a misunderstanding. But the director wouldn't accept her apology. He accused her of being disloyal and unprofessional, accusations that Carla deemed unfair. And he started gossiping about her behind her back, saying that she wasn't a team player and that she was poorly managing the company's public relations effort.

Carla wanted him to stop. This would be a difficult thing to sell.

So she made a plan and outlined how she would approach him. He wasn't accepting her phone calls or responding to her e-mails, so she decided to go directly to his assistant and make an appointment through her.

She examined what kind of support she might need, or if she would need a mediator. So she went to her boss, the company's vice president, to tell him what had happened and what she hoped to accomplish.

She made a bulleted list of points she wanted to make during the meeting. She carefully omitted anything that she thought would make the director defensive. She wanted to explain her point of view and ask him to stop trash-talking her to others around the company.

She also made a list of accusations and objections that he might bring up, and she prepared answers for them. Without that prep, she feared, she might lose her temper or become defensive during the meeting—which she didn't want to happen.

She looked up the director's schedule on the shared company calendar and chose a time when he wasn't busy preparing for travel or important meetings.

And she came up with a Plan B: She would go to human resources with her complaint if the meeting proved unsuccessful.

It didn't. In the end, the two came to an agreement both could live with. Carla's actions were smart. Making a plan, even for a single interaction or transaction, can exponentially improve your chances of success.

2. Who can help you?

The biggest waste of time when you're attempting to make a sale is asking the wrong person.

As you plan for the sale, identify the people who have the authority to make decisions for the company. It doesn't quite make sense to spend a lot of time arguing with a sales clerk when you're trying to return a suit later than the store's policy allows. Instead, ask for the manager, who can override the policy or approve a compromise, like an exchange or a gift card rather than a refund.

Once you identify the authority who can say "yes" to your request, plan the best way to approach her. If you're asking for something that will take time to process, plan to visit the person in the morning rather than during lunch, when she might be taking her only 15-minute break of the day and doesn't want to be disturbed. If you're going to a store or calling a business that deals with a lot of customers, avoid high-traffic times, when the decision maker you need might be extra busy and in no mood to do you a favor.

3. Do you know how to get what you want?

Your plan might include spending time asking experts for advice or attending a training session.

David owns an interior design business and employs a handful of designers and decorators. They each handle their own appointments and market their services mostly via word of mouth.

After about a year of so-so sales, David decided to step up the firm's marketing effort. He directed each of the creative employees on his staff to set up social media accounts and use them to promote their services and show pictures of the homes and offices they have transformed.

A few weeks later, he called a meeting to check in on their progress—and found that nobody was using social media for marketing. The reason: Nobody knew how.

If you expect other people to help you achieve your goals or start selling on your behalf, it's very likely that you will need to teach them how to do it. And you may have to hire an expert or enroll in classes yourself to acquire the skills you need to fulfill your plan.

4. What are your weaknesses?

A plan will help you devise a way to overcome your weaknesses so they don't kill your sale.

When my friend Tanya finally got tired of getting nowhere with the people at human resources over the lack of urgency they had shown in hiring an assistant for her, she made a plan.

Tanya's former assistant had left six months earlier for maternity leave and had decided three months in that she would not return to work. The assistant's work was piling up so high that Tanya was sleeping only four or five hours a night so she could rush to get to the office by 7 a.m. and plow through some of it herself before her daily appointments started.

She made request after request to HR to post the job, recruit candidates, and hire someone to take the assistant's place. The staff there told her several times that a number of staff positions needed filling, and hers wasn't first in line.

Finally, she demanded to be moved to the top of the waiting list.

HR's response? Staffing wasn't a priority at the moment. The company was about to go public, and HR had to update all its policy manuals before the public offering.

Tanya takes things very personally, and that's what she did when she heard the words "not a priority." Losing an assistant, sleep, and her social life, she felt, was enough to make replacing her assistant a priority.

She felt attacked and defeated. She felt like attacking HR in return.

But she realized that wouldn't solve her problem. So she took a breath—and made a plan instead. She decided to plan for how she would "sell" HR on getting her out of her predicament without ruining her reputation with the whole HR staff. A verbal attack didn't seem like a good plan.

Arguing with the HR manager wouldn't have gotten her anywhere; in fact, she would have lost a lot of her power if she had been mean to him. The fact was, she was in the right, so she was in the power position here. It was hers to lose.

When she stepped back and embraced her rational, strategic side, she realized that the HR manager simply did not have the authority to give her what she needed. His mandate was to prep for the upcoming public offering. Replacing an assistant wasn't going to help him do that. So she moved up the ladder to the company's vice president who oversees both Tanya's department and HR. He agreed to meet with Tanya.

Her plan helped her figure out how to go about asking for what she wanted. If she lost her cool during the meeting, she knew that she would not make this "sale" that she was so desperate to make.

She made a plan for what she would say and how she would react if the VP rejected her pleas. She determined in advance what she would accept and what she was willing to compromise on. For instance, she absolutely had to have help and was unwilling to wait any longer. She would even consider working with a temporary assistant until HR had time to find a permanent one. She just needed someone to do the work.

When Tanya was ready for battle, she met with the VP. She was friendly to him. She explained her situation without becoming emotional or angry. She asked very specifically for what she wanted.

And she got it: The VP actually apologized because he didn't know her assistant had decided not to return. He offered her a part-time temp who would work four days a week. And he agreed to direct HR to get a full-time replacement into Tanya's office within four weeks after the public offering.

Tanya didn't say "yes" right away, even though she knew she had already won. Part of her plan was to take a day to look over the backlog of work, consider whether four days a week would cover it, and think about the VP's offer overnight, so she did that. The next day, she accepted the offer.

Her plan worked. She got the help she needed. But it got her something more important: It moved her out of her usual habit of feeling and thinking—and complaining—to acting and doing. It gave her confidence. It gave her a blueprint for the transaction.

5. How confident are you?

A plan will boost your confidence by fully preparing you for the transaction.

Making a sale is like giving a speech: You need to organize your thoughts, know your stuff, rehearse your presentation, and prepare to answer any questions that someone might ask you.

It's likely that the person you are pitching has done his homework, too. So you need to be ultraprepared.

I had to laugh when my friend Terry told me her story about running for Student Government Association treasurer when she was a freshman in high school.

She was running against three other girls. They were to make their cases to the student body at an assembly of about 300 students. They had two weeks' notice.

Terry went first. She stood up intending to tell the audience why she was qualified for the job. But what she didn't count on was becoming dumbstruck the moment the principal handed her the microphone and asked her to make her pitch. She literally had no words because she hadn't prepared a speech. In fact, Terry hadn't taken any time to prepare at all. She hadn't sat down and made a list of qualifications that she could share with the audience in her effort to persuade them to vote for her. She hadn't even considered doing that.

She told me that she has no clue why she didn't prepare. She had never been asked to give a speech before, she said, and she figured she would just get up and talk.

But it turned out she had paralyzing stage fright, brought on, in large part, by her lack of prep.

So she sat down, humiliated and humbled, while the other three candidates delivered their carefully laid-out qualifications for the audience.

This story turns out better than most because Terry won the election, but she only won because her sisters, who also attended the school, got their friends to vote for her. You should never approach a situation the way Terry did and expect a similar outcome. Plan ahead so this never happens to you—because this lesson (that plans result in confidence) was one Terry learned the hard way and never forgot. Don't let it happen to you.

Confidence is important when you're asking others to do something for you. Nothing boosts confidence like thorough preparation in the form of a plan.

Plans can boost your confidence not only for an upcoming transaction, but in general. The more certain you are about what you want and how you plan to achieve it, the more confident you'll feel every day.

SALES CULTURE

No matter which of the 1,100 Firehouse Subs fast-food restaurants around the country you walk into, you'll encounter the same expert sales pitch—from someone who isn't really a salesperson.

The cashier who takes your order will ring up your sandwich, and then ask you, one by one, if you want a drink, chips, a pickle, or dessert. Then the employee will ask you if you want to round up the price of your order to the next dollar as a donation to the Firehouse Subs Safety Foundation, which donates equipment to first responders.

Every time.

So many people say yes to rounding up that the restaurant chain, which was started and is owned by two brothers who are former firefighters, has donated more than $40 million over 20 years in equipment, training, and support to community responders and public safety organizations.

What a great idea. And what great execution.

But imagine if that cashier did not ask you for that spare change. Would you donate it anyway?

What if the cashier asked sometimes but not always? Or if some cashiers asked and others didn't? Or if the company left it up to the cashiers to ask if they feel like it?

My guess is that the company's donations would total far less than $40 million.

The owners, whether they know it or not, have latched onto one of the most important parts of making a plan for selling: Once you decide to sell, do it consistently.

If you're going to get into the habit of asking the customers you work with what else you can sell them, you need to make it a habit. It has to be consistent.

If you're a manager or a team leader or a business owner and you want your nonsales staff to start selling, you have to hold them accountable for it—all of them, not just some—so the effort is consistent. It's part of their culture.

Before I started my professional career, I worked part-time as a cashier at a high-end grocery store that carried gourmet foods, imported beer and wine, and sold other goodies that you don't usually find at the chain markets.

I didn't get any training as a salesperson, but it was crystal clear to me that the customer always came first. If I was busy cleaning up my station or unwrapping quarters for my cash drawer, I was to stop immediately and turn my attention to any customer who approached me. The same was true for the other employees: If someone was slicing meat, cleaning the glass on the bakery display, or pushing a dozen carts from the parking lot to the front of the store, all of that stopped if a customer needed help.

This rule was so consistently enforced that even the owner of the store adhered to it. If someone was wrist-deep in shredding cheese for the salad bar and a customer approached with groceries to check out, the owner would open the register herself so the shopper wouldn't have to wait.

It was so interesting to watch her create a customer-first culture by example. She taught us the rule. She expected everyone to follow the rule. And she followed it herself. She created a culture in which the customers were the priority. No matter what.

That owner understood something that a lot of managers do not: Everyone in that store is a salesperson and an ambassador for the store—cashiers, deli attendants, butchers, bakers, janitors, and the owner.

She made sure we understood it, too.

It worked so well that someone could have come into the shop at any time, without notice, and shot a commercial for the business. We wouldn't have to prepare or pose or put on our best behavior because we always, always behaved the same way at work. We always put the customer first.

So what kind of a commercial are you creating for your business? You create one with your behavior, whether you realize it or not. Is it the one you want to be broadcasting?

If you're an owner, manager, or supervisor, you can and should plan for this kind of "sales" culture. In fact, without a plan, it's unlikely to happen.

I have a client who owns a medium-sized accounting firm and does not employ any official sales professionals. He's an accountant, not a salesperson, officially. His staff consists of accountants, bookkeepers, and an office manager.

They're not salespeople, officially.

They were all pretty good at bringing in new business and soliciting more business from current clients. But they didn't call it sales. Most wouldn't even have considered it sales; they were simply doing what came naturally, and they were doing OK as an organization.

But the owner wanted more than just OK. He wanted to grow the business. He wanted his staff to sell on purpose.

As a result, he invited me to teach all those smart financial professionals my five-step plan for selling. But first, I taught him.

The manager needed to convince the people on his team that sales are not "icky." He needed to show them that they already sell, and they do it successfully. He needed to assure his team that adding "sales" to their jobs would not overburden them; he would hire more staff to help. And finally, he needed to teach them how to sell.

He made a checklist that he wanted them to follow for every single client:

1. Before saying goodbye, ask, "What other questions can I answer for you today?"
2. Ask for a referral to a friend or colleague.
3. Send an e-mail containing a link to an online accountant review site with a request for a positive review.
4. Call the day after the work is done to say thank you.

Nobody could close a job file until all those boxes were checked.

This mandate for consistency was the owner's way of creating a new habit for each employee. It was his way of changing the mindset of the accountants so they would consciously sell.

He even built in celebrations when the firm exceeded its sales goals, and he paid bonuses to staff members who made the most sales.

One problem: After our work together, he didn't continue to enforce it. Bonuses are a great incentive for people who want to earn extra money, but the accountants were already earning a lot, so some of them didn't participate. He had no penalty for those who refused to sell. He did not build selling into the culture of the company.

He's still working on this, but in the meantime, the new system helped the staff increase the number of referrals within two months.

PRO TIP

One of the easiest ways to make a casual, unofficial sale is simply to ask every client or customer, "Is there anything else I can help you with today?" Even better: "Are there any other orders I can open for you today?" Be specific about what else you have to offer.

It's what the cashiers at fast-food restaurants ask: "Do you want fries with that?"

It's what the folks at Firehouse Subs do when they ask for donations: "Would you like to round up to the next dollar?"

It's what you can do every time you work with a client: "What else can I help you with today?"

Simply ask what else your clients need or want, and boom! You're selling. And you're doing it intentionally.

STEP ONE IN ACTION

———————— COMMERCIALS ————————

Have you ever seen a feel-good news story about some random employee who went way above and beyond the call of duty to help out a customer or even someone who wasn't a customer?

Those stories go viral. Maybe it's because there's so much bad news out there that we cling to the nice stories with both hands.

I read a story about a Southwest Airlines employee who personally drove to a traveler's home at 3 a.m. to return a lost suitcase that contained medicine and a rosary that the customer wanted with her at her chemotherapy appointment the next day. Another news item told about a Home Depot employee who helped the parents of a disabled little boy use plumbing pipes to build a makeshift device to help the child practice walking. And a 19-year-old Burger King cashier got a lot of love on social media after a customer snapped her photo while she was escorting an elderly customer to his car after his meal. A Chick-fil-A opened on a Sunday just so a 14-year-old boy could fulfill his dream of working at a drive-through. The store's manager let the child, who has autism and cerebral palsy, hand out cookies to friends and family during his "shift."

No matter how big or small the gesture, kindness always attracts attention.

Kindness sells.

What do you do at work to create a moment that matters for someone? Something that's worthy of a feel-good news story that makes you and your company look good? What have you done lately that would make a good commercial for your business?

The thing about commercial "moments" is that they come from the heart.

And when a business truly puts customers first, those commercials happen every day.

When they do, customers notice. And there's no better sales tool than a culture at work that values service to customers, even when they're not buying anything.

Within a few blocks of my home in San Francisco, three different businesses hand out dog treats to shoppers who stop by while they're walking their pups: a restaurant, a hardware store, and a coffee shop.

My dog, Biscuit, knows where they are, and he leads me to one of the three just about every day.

My favorite is the Cole Hardware store. My husband and I did a major home renovation, so for a while, we constantly needed hardware store-type stuff. Those trips to the hardware store made Biscuit the only one in our house who enjoyed that renovation.

One morning, Biscuit took me to the hardware store on our walk. I hadn't intended to buy anything that day, but Biscuit still got his treat.

I said to the cashier, "This is the best part of my dog's day."

She replied, "No, this is the best part of my day."

I loved that.

What she might not know is this: That was a sales interaction. I could go to another hardware store or to a big-box store to buy my remodeling supplies, but I kept going there because of the dog treats and the way they treated Biscuit and me.

Now that my remodeling project is finished, I still go there—because of what she said. She hands out the treats because she just wants people to stop in and visit. She wants to create a neighborhood atmosphere at the store.

She made me want to go back and give her my business. She made me want to tell people about that store and encourage them to go there.

Wouldn't that make a great commercial?

Most people only talk about their experiences with salespeople when they're negative. We tend to vent about our frustrations.

So I started really trying to notice when someone in sales—or especially someone who's not in sales but winds up selling me on something—does "good."

These feel-good stories are such great examples of how easy it is to sell, simply by being kind and helping others.

The flip side shows us how easy it is to do the opposite of selling—to turn away potential customers.

When you create a negative experience for a customer, you also create a commercial—one that, unfortunately, will replay for a long time.

Here's an example:

I stopped by a gym just to check it out because I walk by it every day when I go to get coffee in the morning, and it looks nice and clean.

You would think the people at the front desk would be trained as salespeople because they're the ones who have to sell you on taking a tour or meeting with a sales rep. Apparently not at this gym.

The person at the front desk didn't seem to have a clue that I might be interested in buying a membership. I asked her if she could give me a schedule of classes. She said no, she didn't have one. I asked her how I could find a schedule. She told me to look online. I asked her if she knew if the gym had a hip-hop aerobics class. She didn't know. She was sitting in front of a computer. She could have looked it up for me.

I asked her if I could pay by the class or if I'd have to buy a full membership. She said I'd have to talk to a sales rep to get that information. I asked her if a sales rep was available. She pointed behind her and said I'd have to ask the trainers sitting at the desks. I didn't. I walked out.

What a missed opportunity. I actually wanted to join a gym. I had planned to join that gym, but I'm not going to bother with one whose employee gave me the impression that nobody there cares enough to help the people who walk in the door.

She could have at least gotten a sales rep to help me. She never offered. She lost the sale and made a bad commercial that I have on replay.

What kind of commercial are you creating with the way you interact with people?

CHAPTER 5

—— STEP TWO ——

Look for Opportunities

YOU'VE PLOWED PRETTY FAR into this book at this point, so I'm going to assume that you're at least somewhat convinced that every job, including yours, is a sales job, at least some of the time.

This chapter will put that conviction to the test.

If you believe that your job is to sell, even if your job description doesn't say a thing about selling, then I might also be able to convince you that it's a good idea for you to look for opportunities to sell. Let's put the sales skills you're learning from this book to the test.

You won't have to look very hard or very long. Opportunities to sell aren't hiding. They're not secret. They're all around you, all the time.

Answer this: Is there something you want? Something you have been dying to ask for but haven't?

Whatever that is, sell it. Sell it to your boss, your colleagues, your clients, your friends, and even the people you meet at those routine corporate receptions.

While reading the previous chapter on planning, you probably spent some time thinking about what you want.

Now it's time to make your wish list. What do you want for yourself at work, in your career, and for your near-term and long-term future? Make a list, and then go after each wish, using the sales skills you're learning from this book.

Here are 10 things that most people who work want—and that they can get if they use the skills of the sales pro: planning, looking for opportunities, establishing trust, asking for what you want, and following up.

1. A raise
2. A promotion or more responsibility
3. A referral from a client or colleague who can introduce you to potential new clients
4. A job, if you don't have one, or a different job if you don't like the one you have
5. A letter of recommendation
6. Praise or at least credit for a job well done
7. A better hotel room or a bigger rental car during a business trip
8. A more convenient shift
9. Time off
10. A bigger office, or a quieter one, or one all to yourself

To get those things, you need to spot your opportunities to sell when they arise. Almost always, those opportunities involve connecting with the people who can move you closer to your goals.

This chapter, "Step Two: Look for Opportunities," is about being alert and networking. It's also about offering what you have that can help people—without being asked.

VIGILANCE

Now that you know that you sell all day long, look for opportunities to do just that. Be vigilant about it and train yourself to notice whenever a window opens. Also, keep this question at the top of your mind at all times: Do I have an opportunity to make an unofficial sale in this situation?

When you ask your boss for a raise or ask a satisfied customer for a reference, you are more likely to hear a "yes" than if you were to keep that question to yourself. The need to be vigilant does not end when you spot the opportunity; instead, you have to keep yourself aware of timing so you know just when to ask.

Get a Raise

If you want something, you need to look for the opportunity to get it. But how do you know when the time is right to ask for it?

For example, if you want a raise, the secret is keeping the idea of "getting a raise" at the top of your mind every day. By doing this, you'll be able to pinpoint the correct moment to ask for one.

To get a raise, you need a plan. Your plan will keep you from blurting out—at just the wrong time—that you resent a coworker who earns more than you or that you believe your boss is playing favorites or taking advantage of you.

Your plan will keep you in check. Your plan will keep you alert and aware so you'll know when it's just the right time to ask for what you want.

Plan to get that raise. Plan to keep your senses sharp for clues that it's the right time to ask. Plan to observe your boss so you'll know when she's in a good mood or when she's likely to bite your head off, even if you just ask to borrow a pencil. Plan to listen carefully whenever she talks about what she wants and needs for her department to be a success.

As with most things in life, the more time you spend planning something, the more likely you are to succeed.

So the big day arrives. The boss has scheduled your performance evaluation. She's in a good mood. At the last department staff meeting, she announced a new project, and she made it clear that this one is super-important to her. She practically pleaded with the staff to handle it with extra care—but to finish it extra quickly. And as it turns out, you don't have any plans for this coming weekend.

Your performance review goes well (as you knew it would), and as the discussion wraps up, you recognize an opportunity. You artfully turn the discussion to the boss's pet project. You show your authentic enthusiasm for it. You acknowledge how important it is to her. You agree that the turnaround time has to be quick, and that will require extra care to avoid errors. You offer to assemble a team to work overtime on Saturday to ease the crunch that could result in overlooking critical details or missing the deadline.

Your offer will remind your boss of your commitment and passion for the job.

The boss is thrilled. You get how important this project is. And you're willing to go the extra mile because you also care not only about the project—but about how important the project is to the boss.

PRO TIP

Showing other people that you genuinely care about something simply because it's important to them will take you far—as long as it's authentic.

You transition back to your performance appraisal and you thank the boss for her kind words and her confidence in you. And right before you leave, you say, "I'm hoping this will help us win this account so we can meet our growth goals. Maybe even translate into a raise for me at my next performance review."

Of course, it's up to the boss, who might plead poverty, bad timing, company policy, or whatever. But you must stick to your plan. You do know you deserve a raise, and you know she knows it, too.

Ask for a Reference

Most people do this one all wrong. They *tell* the boss, colleague, client, or professor that they need a letter of recommendation. Yet the proper way to get one is to politely *ask* for it.

What's your plan? First, choose carefully. Avoid asking for letters from people you have had run-ins with, or who resent you for "stealing" a client away, or whom you haven't been in contact with for so long that they can barely remember what you look like.

This is something I ran into all the time when I was a professor, and I still encounter it occasionally since I opened my own consulting company. And I'm definitely not the only one.

A former colleague was telling me the other day about a young woman who asked her for a letter of recommendation for an internship. The professor, who is usually happy to recommend her students—as she truly wishes them success—said she had to think about how to respond to this former student for a full two days.

One year earlier, the student had totally lost it in class while learning a new software program. She got frustrated, called the teacher over, and literally yelled, "This is stupid!" followed by a few other accusations, and then she stormed out of the computer lab so she could hide in the women's room while she sobbed.

A year later, she asked this professor to recommend her for an important internship. The professor politely refused, saying simply that it would be better for the student to find another instructor to write the letter.

"Why?" the student e-mailed her.

The professor recounted the incident.

The student, who frequently saw the professor in the hallway between classes, had never apologized for her outburst, and, in fact, had never said a word to my colleague since the class ended.

That student made a few missteps here. It was as if she didn't even know how upsetting her outburst was to the professor and to her classmates. Or if she did know, she figured a teacher couldn't say no to a request for a letter of recommendation.

What benefit would the professor possibly get from writing that letter? I can't think of any.

In this situation, nobody wins.

——————— ———————

Sometimes you can get a reference without even asking, too. I know this from experience, because I have referred Delta Air Lines to a ton of friends and clients after a great experience I had on a trip with Delta.

I'm always cold—even in July—and especially in winter, even when the heat is turned up full blast. I think it's because I'm from the South, where it's always pretty warm. On one particular Delta flight, I felt like I was about to freeze to death—and for the record I am well aware of my low tolerance, so I dressed accordingly in long pants, a sweater, a jacket, and a scarf.

This flight was incredibly cold, more so than usual. I dug into my carry-on bag, pulled out my winter coat, draped it over my body, and curled up under the little airplane blanket I took from the overhead bin. I was bundled up from nose to toes, but still freezing. So much so that I asked the flight attendant to bring me another blanket and ask the pilot to turn the air conditioning off.

She came back empty-handed, on both accounts. Apparently, the air conditioning was broken, so it was freezing in the front of the plane and uncomfortably hot in the back. And she was fresh out of blankets.

Still, she offered to move me to the tropics at the back of the plane, but I would have had to squeeze into a middle seat between two travelers who were probably complaining about the heat as much as I was whining about the cold.

She brought me a cup of hot coffee. She came back with refills several times. She distracted me from my discomfort by sticking around and having a conversation with me. And she added a bunch of unearned airline miles to my Delta account.

She went over and beyond. She saw an opportunity to turn a pretty miserable flight into a tolerable one.

The things that were in her control, she did.

Even though I had a rough trip, I left the plane with a good feeling and gave the flight attendant some love on social media and a great review on the airline's follow-up survey.

Take Action

My friend Ruthie is an architect who designs small office buildings in a small Northeastern city. The builders don't like the building owners spending too much time on the construction site for safety reasons. But a lot of owners are very nervous about how much progress everyone is making during construction, and they insist they need to see for themselves.

Ruthie takes photos of the progress every couple of days and shares them with the owners. But sometimes, they're still not satisfied.

She doesn't want to lose those clients—they bring her a lot of repeat business and send a lot of referrals. But she also doesn't want them walking around a dangerous construction site.

One day, she opened an e-mail that had come to her by way of a listserv she was on because she had taught an architecture class at a nearby community college a couple of times. The message was about a new program at the college to teach people how to fly drones and prepare them to take a required Federal Aviation Administration test that would qualify them as drone pilots.

When Ruthie saw that, a light bulb came on: If she could fly drones over the offices as they were in various stages of construction, she could take videos and photos of the framing inside a building's exterior walls, even before the roof goes on. That way, an owner could get a look at how big the rooms are and exactly where they are located.

Her challenge: Getting into the training. It was only for professors, and she was a part-time adjunct who hadn't taught there in two years. Her plan: Try anyway.

She made a plan. She researched the ways architects have used drones to help their businesses, and she read about the college's mission to contribute to the success of the community outside campus. Then she made her pitch to the lead trainer, who allowed her into the class.

A day earlier, it would never have occurred to Ruthie to sell herself as a future drone pilot. But now not only does she photograph her own projects, but she rents herself out as a drone photographer to other architects and builders in her community.

And during the many media interviews she has given since she started using her drone, she gives the college credit by talking about the training she got.

Win-win.

NETWORKING

One of my rules of thumb is, "You can't do it alone." No one can.

By "it," I mean life. Career. Work-life balance. All of it.

And the best people to help you often are the people closest to you: family, friends, colleagues, and business associates.

My friend Kierstan found this out at a Valentine's Day dance. She belonged to a professional organization for women in graphic design that held a heart-themed gala to raise money for the group.

Funny thing about that gala: Only women attended. Kierstan and the other organizers thought everyone would bring their Valentines, but they didn't.

So the women used the opportunity to get to know each other better.

Kierstan used it to score a huge freelance job.

She and an acquaintance, Eve, were goofing off together on the dance floor, trying out some old disco moves they had seen in a 1970s movie. Afterward, as they shared some punch, Kierstan told Eve about her decision to quit her job in the marketing department of a big company and hang out her shingle as a full-time freelance graphic designer.

She came right out and asked Eve, who heads the marketing department at another firm, if her company could use her services as a freelancer.

Eve explained, "Unfortunately, all of our people are full time. We never use freelancers."

Kierstan handed her a business card anyway, and said, "Well, if you ever change your mind, here's how to contact me."

A few weeks later, Eve did just that. A graphic designer at her office had to go out for a couple of months on medical leave, and Eve thought of Kierstan.

That was 10 years ago, and Kierstan still fills in for all the graphic designers at Eve's company whenever they're on vacation or out sick.

That's what networking can get you. Take advantage of it.

Not much of a mingler?

I'll share a secret with you: Even though people tell me I'm friendly and outgoing, and I generally like people, I'm not much of a mingler, either.

I feel like the kind of talking we do at social events and conferences is mostly just chitchat, and I prefer to really get to know people on a more personal and deeper level.

But I have to say, those receptions have helped me land a lot of business for my company. They have made it possible for me to meet people I otherwise would never have met. They give me an opportunity to tell people about my company, Orange Leaf Consulting.

I've come up with a foolproof, seven-part system for getting in, making as many valuable contacts as I can, and getting out that I'd like to share with you now.

Eight Networking Secrets

1. **Go.** Even if you hate business receptions, or company picnics, or client lunches, show up. You can't

make contacts if you don't meet people. You can't make unofficial sales for your company if you don't talk to people who might want to do business with you. You can't build your own reputation and sell yourself if you never leave your cubicle.

2. **Have fun, even if you're faking it.** Force yourself to smile, and pretty soon, you'll feel like smiling. If you smile, people will be way, way more likely to approach you, take an interest in you, and even say "yes" to you when your company has a product or a service that can solve your new friend's problem.

3. **Talk.** You aren't the only one who would rather have a root canal than spend an evening floating around a room full of people you barely know. So a lot of the people you meet there aren't going to know what to say, either. Or are too shy to say anything. Or are waiting for you to start the conversation. Do it. Learn the skill of small talk. More on this in Chapter 6, which focuses on talking and listening.

4. **Watch your words.** I hope you already know that you should never talk about politics, religion, or sex with people at a work function. Stick with topics that everyone likes to talk about: the weather, the latest movies you've seen, the day's nonpolitical news. When you meet someone new or reconnect with someone you've met a couple of times already, ask about the person's job and family and vacation.

5. **Listen for clues.** The other person might have a need or a desire for something your company has to

offer. Stock your wallet with business cards before you arrive at the event. Hand them out liberally, but don't push anything on anyone. Instead, how about inviting the other person to connect again over lunch or via phone the following week? A second meeting is a giant leap forward in the world of sales. It will give you an opportunity to talk privately and in more depth about how you can help the other person out.

6. **Take breaks.** I do it all the time. I'll talk to three people, and then I'll excuse myself and visit the restroom or go somewhere to check my phone. I go back to the party and talk to three more and then slip away to get some fresh air. After that, I chat with three final people, and then I call it a night.

7. **Exit gracefully.** Don't get trapped in a long, dragged-out debate or conversation. Say a few words, and then politely excuse yourself. Then slip away without making a big deal out of it. Say you see someone you know. Tell the other person you're headed to the bar and offer to bring back a drink. Or make an excuse, like, "I've got to make a quick call. I'll see you later." Then walk away. It works. It's not rude, and it's not so hard, is it? When it's time to leave the party, go.

8. **Give yourself an "end" time.** I'll decide ahead of time that I will only stay an hour, and then I'm out. Receptions and other work functions really aren't a forum for getting into deep conversations or making lifelong friends. They're more about small talk,

seeing and being seen, meeting people, and perhaps arranging for a second meeting later.

OFFERING

I ordered a salad to go the other day at a really busy sandwich shop that makes more sandwiches than salads and I wound up waiting about 15 minutes to get my lunch.

I stood next to the cashier as I waited. I watched customer after customer order their sandwiches and chips, pay, and sit down. Then I watched those same customers come back to the cashier, one after the other, to place a second order—for something to drink.

One of them was a young mother with a baby and a toddler. The poor woman had taken her kids and her food to an empty table, strapped the baby into a high chair, unpacked the sandwiches, tied bibs around the kids' necks, and taken her seat. Before she could exhale, she realized she hadn't ordered any drinks.

So she unbuckled the baby and picked her up, took the toddler by the hand, prayed that nobody would mess with the lunch she had already spread out on the table, and made her way to the counter to order a large lemonade and a bottle of apple juice.

It prompted me to say something to the 16-year-old cashier who hadn't figured this out herself: I suggested that she ask every single customer who orders food if he or she would like to also buy a drink.

She loved that idea, but it simply had never occurred to her. And it hadn't occurred to her manager, either. The manager had taught her about how to make sandwiches, count change, and clock in and out, but nobody taught her how to sell.

I watched as she tried it out, and nearly 100 percent of the customers over the next 10 minutes or so said yes to drinks.

I told the cashier the same thing I'm telling you: Selling is about filling someone else's need. This teenager could have saved that young mother a lot of hassle and upset—and perhaps even given her a moment of peace during a stressful day out with two little ones—if she had simply offered to sell the woman something she needed anyway.

For people who took their lunch to go, she could save them from having to eat their sandwiches without a drink to help wash them down. For those who might place large orders, reminding them to buy drinks might result in making them heroes back at the office because their colleagues wouldn't have to forage around to get coffee or buy soft drinks from vending machines.

Her job is to take orders and collect money. She's not officially a salesperson, but if she offers to sell drinks, she brings in more money for the shop, makes her boss happy, and fulfills a need for people to drink when they eat.

My point: Don't wait for people to ask you for what they want. Instead, figure out what they want and offer it. It's easy to do.

I told you about my air-conditioning tech, Ben, who reacted to an offhand comment I made about my furnace by offering to take a look at it—which added a furnace repair job to the air-conditioning maintenance he was there to do.

My neighbor told me about a similar experience. Her husband wasn't up for hanging the holiday lights on their two-story house last Christmas. Everyone in the neighborhood noticed the missing lights because the couple lived on the corner and had always sort of overdone the icicle lights every year.

A guy who lived down the street from them—my friend didn't even know him—noticed, too. So he stopped by, introduced himself as a roofer, and said the roofing company he worked for was in the business of hanging holiday lights in the winter. She hired him on the spot.

This roofer isn't a salesperson by trade or by training: He's a roofer. But he saw that his neighbor needed help, and he knew his company could help her.

He made the sale. His boss was happy. My neighbor got her lights up. Her husband stopped feeling guilty. The neighbors didn't have to stop gossiping about the gaudy house on the corner.

Win-win-win-win-win. Selling fills needs. It helps others. It feels good to help others.

———————   ———————

Start to look for opportunities to offer to help people. An accountant who simply walks across the street before getting into his car so he can help an elderly woman pull her trash cans back to the house on garbage collection day might not seem like he's selling something. But that kindness—any kindness, really—could go a long way toward building his reputation as a caring, helpful person.

Then, the next time that neighbor's daughter is struggling with her taxes, finding them too complicated to do by herself, and complains to her mother about them, that elderly woman is going to recommend the very kind accountant who lives across the street.

Sale.

My friend Suze and her husband like to take long weekends a few times a year and travel to big cities, like New York and Chicago. Suze never really cared which hotel she stayed in, as long as the location and price were right.

But a year or so ago, the couple decided to go to New York for Christmas, and she had a hard time finding an available room online at a price she could afford. She searched hotel after hotel, and every website basically said, "No vacancy," and that was that.

So she went the old-fashioned route: She made a phone call to Hilton's reservation desk. The operator confirmed that the specific hotel Suze wanted to stay in was already booked for the holiday, but she also offered to search the whole city for vacancies in her price range. The operator worked with Suze for a good 20 minutes and found four suitable rooms. Suze booked on the spot.

So that operator made a sale—that's sort of her job, isn't it?

But here's what happened: Suze and her husband now only stay at Hiltons. They signed up for the chain's honors program, got Hilton credit cards, and are now brand-loyal.

That operator not only sold Suze a hotel room for her weekend in New York. She sold Suze on becoming a loyal customer for life—in just 20 minutes. How's that for a return on investment? A 20-minute conversation turned Suze into a customer for life.

All the operator had to do was offer. You can do that, too. Train yourself to listen for opportunities. To hear it when someone tells you she needs something—even if it's an offhand remark. Even if it's unrelated to what the two of you are talking about. Even if you're doing unrelated business with this person.

If someone complains or indicates a lack of something: Hear that.

Quickly run through ways you or your business can fill that lack; tell the person what you have to offer that might help.

Train yourself to pay attention. Recognize when a door is opening.

And then walk through.

Many times, walking through means offering without being asked—and you should be ready in case someone does ask.

One of my favorite stories where this played out in a memorable way involves the actor who played Gunther on the sitcom *Friends*.

For a year and a half, James Michael Tyler's nameless character silently poured coffee and pined away for the beautiful Rachel, never saying a word. During the middle of the second season, though, one of the show's executives asked him if he had any acting experience. He certainly did, and he said so.

He was ready to offer his services as soon as the opportunity presented itself. He was ready to make the sale.

And he did make the sale. His character got a name and lines to recite. Tyler kept that role throughout the rest of the show's 10-year run.

Be ready.

Spot opportunities. Seize them. Speak up. Make the sale.

STEP TWO IN ACTION

—— MOMENTS THAT MATTER ——

Any time you happen to talk to another person about your job or your company, you have the opportunity to make a sale. Any time you come into contact with a client, customer, or even a random member of the public while you're working, you have the opportunity to make a sale.

That's true whether your official job title or job description has anything to do with sales or not. So it baffles me to no end on the occasions when I go shopping and feel unappreciated by the salespeople who are supposed to help me.

The most memorable example of this that I can recall comes from my friend Freda, who is a self-confessed shopaholic. She loves one particular department store—a huge chain that carries dresses in all her favorite brands.

Freda shops there frequently, both in the store and online. The chain has three stores near her—one close to home, one a few miles from work, and one that's across the street from a client's office that she visits nearly every week.

But for the past six months or so, she has stopped shopping there—cold turkey. You're not going to believe this story. I still can't believe it.

After a client appointment, she walked over to the store, as she usually did. She had ordered a dress online that turned out to be a bit snug, so she wanted to exchange it in the store for one in a bigger size.

She had exchanged online purchases at this store many times.

Unfortunately, the store only had her size in purple, and the dress she was returning was green. She decided to go for the purple one and took both dresses, plus another one she had tried on, to the register. Freda was ready to buy.

The cashier said she couldn't make the exchange because the purple one cost more than the green one.

So Freda asked if she would be able to make the exchange anyway, as the store did not have the green one. The cashier said "no."

She didn't hesitate to say no, either. She didn't say, "I wish I could, but I'm not allowed to." Or ask if she could try to find the green one in another store or online and have it shipped. Or offer to ask a manager to make an exception because the store was out of the green one. She just said "no."

So Freda decided to buy the dress online in the right size and asked if she could return the snug green dress at the store.

Again, the cashier said no.

After another 20 minutes of my friend going back and forth with this person in order to get a refund, she finally asked for a manager; the cashier said there wasn't one in the store at that time.

Frustrated, my friend simply asked her to ring up the second dress she had brought to the register. After the transaction was done, Freda said, "I'll say 'you're welcome' even though you didn't say 'thank you.'"

To that, the cashier responded—I kid you not— "Why would I thank you?"

My friend said, "Because I just made a purchase at the store you work for."

And the cashier actually laughed out loud.

Are you as flabbergasted by this story as I am?

My friend was upset enough to take another half hour out of her day to find the store manager's office to report what had happened. The manager apologized, said she would speak to the cashier, and processed the refund for the green dress.

My friend hasn't been back to that store—her favorite store—since this incident. In fact, she hasn't been back to any other store in that chain since.

I talk a lot in this book about creating a "customer for life." This experience—this awful, wasted hour—turned my friend from a customer for life into the customer of a competitor in just a few moments.

———————   ———————

Selling is all about creating moments. My friend Phylecia calls them "moments that matter." What I've described is a moment that mattered so much to my friend that she has turned her back on her favorite store.

That's not the kind of moment you'll want to create if you're trying to do a good job for your company. Or impress your boss. Or be a helpful person. Or simply treat people right.

Moments that matter should be good experiences for the person who encounters you as a representative of your employer.

Again, remember Ben, the HVAC tech who came to fix my air conditioner and wound up taking care of my furnace at the same time? That was a moment that mattered to me. That was an unexpected kindness that saved me money and hassle and time. That was a gesture that turned me into a customer of his company for life.

Here's a moment that mattered to my friend Christy so much that it helped her decide which company to work for.

She had traveled to Silicon Valley for job interviews with a couple of huge tech companies. She's a digital whiz, and she had been heavily recruited by a number of prestigious companies that pay enormous salaries so they can attract the best and the brightest.

She actually wound up in the middle of an unbelievable bidding war between these two companies, which were both offering her sky-high signing bonuses, fancy offices, and fulfilling work.

It was the tiniest incident that weighed the heaviest as she made her decision.

Both of these companies are located on vast campuses. They're so big and have so many employees that they need several buildings to fit them all.

When Christy arrived on the first campus, she got lost.

She was roaming around trying to find a building and stopped someone who looked like he knew where he was headed. She asked for directions, but he didn't know the building she was looking for and kept walking. She stopped a second employee, who pointed to the left and said, "Keep walking that way. You'll find it eventually." She didn't—and she was 10 minutes late for her appointment.

For the interview at the second company, she arrived an hour early, anticipating she would be on her own again when it came time to navigate the oversized campus. She got lost again, but this time she stopped a security guard and asked for directions. He looked like he was in a hurry, so she braced for the "no." To her surprise, he stopped, laughed, and said he had worked there for two years and still got lost sometimes. He said her destination was two buildings away, and she would never find it on her own.

"Come on. I'll walk you over there," he said.

"Won't you be late?" she asked. "You seemed like you were in a hurry."

"We're never in too much of a hurry to help a visitor," he said.

He delivered her to the front door of the building she was looking for and wished her luck with her interview. He handed her his business card and invited her to call him if she took the job.

She took the job at the second company, and the two of them have lunch every few weeks now that they're colleagues.

Christy had memorable moments at each company. But they were memorable for very different reasons.

Both were moments that matter.

What kind of moments are you creating when you interact with people who are or could be customers of your company?

People remember moments. A good experience will shape a stranger's perception of you and your business. A bad experience will do the same.

Which experience are you offering?

Often, it's the smallest things that make the biggest difference. When you notice that a wedding dress sparkles, for instance, it's because of the hundreds of minuscule sequins that someone took the time to sew into it. Those are tiny little things that give the impression of something bigger. When you take care with the little things, those pieces come together. When you create a special moment, someone will remember it—and you—forever.

And when you wreck a special moment, that will be remembered, too.

One of the nicest things my husband ever did for me was to plan a special day for me in New York City.

We don't splurge that often, so when we do, we want to make it worth every penny. That year for Christmas, he ordered me a gorgeous bracelet from a haute New York jeweler, but that wasn't even the nicest thing.

He also brought me to New York and checked us into a beautiful hotel for the weekend. He scheduled a very New York-y day for us: lunch at my favorite deli, ice skating at Rockefeller Center, a glass of champagne at the Plaza hotel—followed by a trip to pick up my fancy bracelet.

Mid-day, we walked to the shop, waited for a few minutes in line, and told the salesperson that we were there to pick up an item that we had ordered. She disappeared, and moments later, she came back with my gift from the safe.

She was carrying a tiny box with a beautiful bow wrapped around it. Inside was a velvet lining and a velvet pouch, and inside the pouch was my stunning new bracelet.

As she presented the box, I couldn't wait to open it. I wanted to rip it open, but I had planned earlier that I would unwrap everything very slowly so I could savor the experience.

I didn't get the chance.

Instead, the woman yanked the bow off the box, opened it, emptied the bracelet out of the pouch, and handed it to me.

She completely stole my moment. We were dumbfounded, and she could tell.

"Is something wrong with the bracelet?" she asked.

She had no clue that she had completely ruined my moment—and missed her own, too.

It's not often that I get a present like that. When I do, it's a special treat for a special occasion, but to that salesperson it was just a transaction. I still love my bracelet, but I won't buy another from that jeweler.

CHAPTER 6

—— STEP THREE ——

Establish Trust

THE KEY TO MY five-step sales process for nonsales-people is this: If you want something from someone, figure out what that person will get in return. To do this, you have to get to know the person a little bit and establish trust between the two of you. Someone who trusts you is more likely to help you than someone who doesn't.

Trust isn't automatic. You can spend time with someone without building trust. You can strike a rapport without building trust.

I can like you and still not trust you. I can even hang out with you and still not trust you.

Establishing trust starts with you taking a genuine interest in another person. You need to listen in earnest when that person shares information and feelings with you. You need to observe the person's situation to determine if you have something to offer that can improve it. You need to talk enough to let the person know you understand him or her, but don't talk so much that you make the interaction only about you. And you need to behave in a way—consistently—that shows the person that you walk your own talk, that you are kind and ethical, and that you will honor any promises you might make as you negotiate your unofficial sale.

This step, "Establish Trust," is about doing those four things: listen authentically, observe, talk, and behave.

LISTEN

I was impressed with Pauline, an employee of a client of mine who decided she wanted and deserved more of an annual pay raise than she had been offered. She had marched right into her boss's office—the office of my client—and said so.

Unfortunately, my client told Pauline that money had been tight over the past few months and that the raises he had already offered to employees were all he could afford.

Pauline gently objected to his lumping her in with all the other employees, and she explained how she had excelled at her job over the past year and had contributed in no small measure to the company's slow climb out of a rough few seasons.

She believed her base salary was at least $7,500 too low, and she wanted to stay at my client's firm, but she needed him to, as she put it, "make her whole." Pauline's boss was worried that one of his most valuable employees would leave the company, and he didn't want that. Still, he said he couldn't come up with money he didn't have. So he assured Pauline that next year would be a better time to negotiate a bigger salary bump.

What Pauline did next was brilliant, and it got her even more than what she wanted. And she couldn't have gotten it if she hadn't been listening carefully and with an open mind as my client spoke to her.

"I understand that money is tight this year and that next year will be better for the company," she repeated to my client. "Let me propose a solution that will work for both of us."

She laid out a three-year plan for staggered pay raises equal to more than $12,000 instead of just $7,500: $2,250 this year, $5,250 next year, and a $5,000 bonus on top of the "normal" raise the year after that in exchange for her promise not to take a job anywhere else for three years. She proposed that the human resources department would draw up a contract for her and my client to sign.

My client agreed to those terms. The pair shook hands, and they both left the meeting with smiles on their faces.

Pauline succeeded in this negotiation because she listened to what my client was saying: He simply did not have the money this year, but next year he would. She succeeded because she had a plan and didn't give up the first time she heard a "no." She succeeded because she figured out that my client valued her as an employee and wanted to retain her, but he didn't know how to do what she was asking, given this year's tight purse strings.

She sold my client on a $12,000-plus raise by listening until she understood what he wanted and what he was able—and not able—to do. She sold my client by giving him something—a chance to retain her without coming up with $7,500 this year.

She got what she wanted and then some. He got what he wanted and then some. She made the sale.

My Southern aunt used to say that God gave us two ears and one mouth for a good reason: We should listen twice as much as we talk.

That's never truer than when you're trying to get someone to give you something you want. You need to listen hard enough to hear why someone is saying yes, no, or maybe. You need to listen hard enough to hear what you can do for him in order to get him to do something for you.

Most people only half-listen. We get distracted. We interrupt a conversation to read a text. We formulate what we want to say while the other person is talking.

Yet there's no way except by actively listening to truly understand how you can fill another person's need. And if you can't help the other person somehow, your chances that he or she will help you greatly diminish.

PRO TIP

Listening is the secret to selling anything.

Listening is what you should do before you ever utter a word; before you ask for what you want; before you jump to any conclusions.

In fact, what you say should be a response to what the other person has already said. It should never be a rehearsed spiel that only takes into account what you want. What you say should address how you can help the other person. You can't possibly address that if you don't know what the other person needs.

Listening will clue you in.

Here's what you'll hear: Is the person in a good mood—good enough to say "yes" to your request? Is this a good time to ask, or would later be better? Is there something you can do or say that will make the other person more likely to help you out?

You'll hear if there's a reason why the person will want to help you with your specific request—or not. Listening will help you collect the information you need so that when it's your turn to talk, you'll say just the right thing. You'll ask in just the right way.

If you listen before you talk, what you say is a response. What you say will address what the other person has told you. What you say will be about the other person, not about you. What you say will tell the other person if you have something that will help him or her. It will let the other person know that you have something that can meet a need that you learned about because you cared enough to listen.

When you listen, it establishes goodwill, warm feelings, and trust. It's simple: Listen first; then respond. In that order. A lot of professional salespeople are terrible at this—and aren't successful as a result.

Some sales pros are just too aggressive. They talk your ear off about their product or service, even though they have no clue if you need it or want it. They tell you why you should buy it, but they really don't know if you need it.

Make listening the first thing you do even when you can't wait to tell people how they can help you. It's the secret to getting what you want: a new client, a second meeting, a deal, a raise, a bigger hotel room, a meeting with a busy manager.

Truly listen. Listen to understand. Listen to empathize. Listen because you're authentically interested.

The secret to my success in sales is that I genuinely care about what the other person has to say. The secret to my success as a consultant and sales trainer: I authentically care about helping my clients.

- I listen not because I have to, but because I want to.
- I am naturally curious, and I really care about helping people.
- And people trust me. Establishing trust is the way to "yes."

Establishing trust means clients believe I would never sell them something they don't need or want. That's my personal commitment to them. That's my personal brand.

If you have to pretend to be interested, people will know. Your eyes, your tone of voice, and your responses will reveal that you're faking it.

If you hear a story you can relate to, say so. Empathize. Share your own story so the other person will know that you really do understand.

If someone is upset and frazzled after a long day of hearing complaints from frustrated customers, recall the day when that happened to you. Tell the person you've been there. Tell her you're not going to complain. Tell her she's doing a great job of handling it.

She might be the hotel clerk, the receptionist at the company where you have a meeting, the hostess in a restaurant where you're taking clients to lunch, or your company's IT tech on the other end of the phone. No matter who it is or what you need, listen first; then respond and empathize.

Best practices:

- **Give.** Then get.
- **Ask.** Don't demand.
- **Listen first.** Then respond.
- **Be authentic.** Establish trust.

OBSERVE

This story is funny now, but it was anything but on the day my friend Carly had the opportunity of a lifetime to get a venture capitalist to invest in an office-sharing company she had just started. ·

A born entrepreneur, Carly had spent a decade working for other start-ups, learning the ins and outs of creating a business from nothing. About six months earlier, she had opened a small office and recruited a handful of lawyers, teleworkers, and other professionals to lease desks, clerical help, copying services, and a receptionist as needed.

The venture was successful, and she wanted to expand, so she approached investors, and after a dozen or so "no thank you" responses, she finally had some interest from a well-known, well-funded VC company.

She scheduled her pitch for Friday morning.

The guy showed up with a colossal hangover. He was guzzling water, popping aspirins as if they were breath mints, and rubbing his eyes. He complained that he wasn't feeling well but encouraged her to go ahead and make her pitch.

Bold as it was to do this, Carly said no. She knew this was her big chance, and yet she didn't stand a chance if she pitched to this investor in his condition.

She politely offered sympathy that the investor wasn't feeling well, and firmly—but nicely—suggested that they reschedule for a morning when he would be less distracted. He reluctantly admitted that she was right.

It was the wrong time to have this discussion. He was in no shape to listen or negotiate.

She called him the next Monday to reschedule. Embarrassed, he excused his behavior as the flu and agreed to another meeting.

———————   ———————

Sizing up a person and the circumstances you find your-self in is an important step to take before you ask someone for his business, for a favor, or for a raise. Sometimes, it's just not a good time.

Sometimes, the person doesn't have the authority to say yes. Sometimes, you already know the answer is going to be "no."

Before you ever ask anyone for anything, size up the person and the situation. Change your plan if you can tell it's not going to go well for you.

By now, you know the process of getting what you want—what I call selling—isn't about you. Instead, it's about understanding how what you're selling could be valuable to the person you're trying to sell to. It's about figuring out what you have that might be valuable to the other person. It's a trade. It's about creating a win for both you and the person you hope will help you.

Just as listening will help you figure out what you can do for the other person, sizing him or her up will help you determine whether to ask and how to ask.

This is an important step. Few things are more disap-pointing than hearing a "no" because you asked at just the wrong time. Or you asked the wrong person.

It's a step that reinforces the core concept of my five-step sales process for nonsalespeople: Selling is as much about giving as it is about getting.

Notice what people are doing before you decide whether to ask them for help, a favor, an appointment, a raise, or anything else.

And realize that when it comes to how you should approach someone with a request, one size definitely does not fit all.

Danielle supervised a staff of eight people. She really needed help with her management style. She had an office with a door, and each of her staff worked in a cubicle nearby.

Danielle is a driven person. When she has a task to finish, she puts her head down and doesn't look up until the task is complete. If she has a busy day ahead of her, she makes a beeline from the elevator to her office and shuts the door so she can get started and work without interruptions.

The problem with that routine, of course, is that she's supposed to be supervising eight people. With her door closed and her eyes on her computer, she wasn't paying any attention to them.

She didn't even say "good morning" to them as she walked past them to her office.

They often needed her input, but they were generally afraid to interrupt her when she was in her zone. They had observed that she would appear bothered and too busy if they did, but they really needed her.

So the team got together and came up with a plan. Donald—a senior member of the team and someone Danielle obviously liked and trusted—approached her to explain the problem and suggested a system. On days when the staff felt scared to approach her because of her demeanor, Donald would knock on the door and ask, "Are you OK?" That would be code for "Why aren't you speaking to us? Did we do something wrong? Is it OK for us to come in and ask for help today?"

And that's how the team sized Danielle up from then on. If anyone needed help, had a question, wanted to complain, or had a reason to engage with Danielle on one of her "focused" days, Donald would knock on her door first and ask if she was OK. And she would let him know if it was safe for the others to approach.

The fact is, there's no point approaching someone to ask for a favor if the person clearly isn't in the mood to hear from you. Size her up first.

PRO TIP

It's important to connect with the people you work with, and being approachable is an important part of that. When people feel safe and know they can be themselves around you, that builds trust.

Oh, and for the record, if Danielle were one of my clients, I would have coached her on how to be more approachable.

Sometimes, if you're a keen observer, you can change someone's mood from tense to cooperative.

I booked a hotel room for a five-day business trip not long ago. When I arrived, one receptionist was behind the desk, and about 15 people were waiting in line to check in. I was hoping to convince the receptionist to upgrade my room to a larger one with a kitchenette.

So I sized up the situation. With 15 people in line ahead of me, that receptionist would most likely be tired and frazzled by the time it was my turn. What could I do to bring her around to a "yes"—or should I even bother trying?

I could see that the receptionist was having a hectic hour. I observed that she was tired and stressed out and wasn't really making eye contact with the guests. Like Danielle, she had her head down and was focused on checking people in as efficiently as possible. She seemed to be in sort of a bad mood.

Maybe I shouldn't have asked for anything, but I figured I would give it a shot. I knew I should ask nicely, as I never try to steamroll people. That just doesn't work for me. I don't demand. And I don't make it about me.

This was going to be about her.

It was my turn. I commented on how busy she was, and she acknowledged that it was an especially busy afternoon.

I complimented her on how she was handling it. I told her I would be snapping at people if I were in her place, and she said she had to hold herself back.

"You're a better woman than I am," I told her.

She smiled. I smiled back.

I think she needed a moment of levity. That's what she needed from me. Her mood lightened.

I told her that I was going to be staying for five days and that the two of us would be seeing a lot of each other. She smiled again.

I asked for the upgrade. I asked if she could do that for me. I showed her that I knew she had the authority and that she would be doing me a huge favor.

She actually said "yes." But even if she hadn't, at least I tried.

If I hadn't been able to make her smile, I wouldn't have asked her for anything extra. I might have waited until there was a shift change and another receptionist, one who hadn't been checking in guests for eight hours, could help me out.

It's about sizing things up. Here's how:

- **Observe before you speak.** Take a minute to assess the situation, the person's mood, and your chances for a "yes."
- **Truly make it about the other person.** Make small talk that's about the person and her circumstances.
- **Consider what you can "trade."** Could the receptionist use a compliment? An acknowledgment of how hard she's working and what a good job she's doing? Or an encounter with someone who would simply be nice to her? Even if she doesn't agree to the free upgrade, you might just make her day. Just doing that gives you a great reward.

- **Check out the person's body language.** Is her smile genuine or fake? Does she make eye contact? Does she seem interested in helping the hotel guests or just in getting them out of the lobby?
- **Is this really the best time to ask?** Does the person look like she's having a bad day? Is there a huge line of people waiting?
- **Is this really the right person to ask?** Asking the wrong person isn't going to get you what you want.

You can size up people every time you have the opportunity to "sell" in a business or personal situation.

TALK

Listening and observing before talking will make what you say more meaningful and relevant to the other person. But you might have to get the conversation going first.

Your opportunities to make unofficial sales for yourself or your company will often come about when you're talking to a stranger or to someone you don't know well.

So by way of introduction, you have to make small talk.

I love small talk, at least in small doses. People tell me that I've never met a stranger and that I can talk to anyone about anything. I guess that's because I'm genuinely curious about people and interested in their stories.

I talk to people at the grocery store, in the line at Starbucks, at the airport, in the elevator—everywhere. I sit up front with my Lyft driver so we can have a running conversation all through the trip. I chat with people at work functions and at parties. And to tell you the truth, I get a lot of business for my company that way. I get a lot of business for my company because I ask people to tell me their stories. And I tell them mine.

To establish trust, you have to listen and observe. You also have to talk.

My hairdresser is a master of small talk. When I first met him, we were in an airport.

I have long, very curly blonde hair. I was waiting in line to board a plane for home—I had just moved to San Francisco—and he asked me who colors my hair.

I chuckled. It's natural.

He said he was a hairdresser and handed me his card. We chatted about San Francisco, and I told him I didn't know anyone there yet.

He said, "You do now." He's been my hairdresser for 14 years—and my friend.

Talking will help you establish trust and confidence, even if it's with a stranger. The sooner you learn to chit-chat with people you don't know, the sooner you will find your opportunities expand.

———————   ———————

At a trade show and convention I attended not too long ago, a colleague and I stopped by a reception with about 300 participants. My friend is uncomfortable in those situations, so he found a seat and sat there nursing a glass of wine for an hour while I made the rounds.

By the end of the evening, I had collected about a dozen business cards from people I had chatted with about my company and about their companies. I made a few follow-up calls when I got back to work, and two weeks later, one of those people hired my firm to help teach his company's nonselling team members how they can bring in more business by recognizing opportunities to make unofficial sales.

My friend didn't collect any business cards, so he didn't have anyone to follow up with later. All he got out of that reception was a glass of wine.

It takes more than small talk to establish trust, of course. But chitchat can begin a conversation that can lead to a productive business relationship. It's the first step.

So take the first step: Talk to a stranger.

You don't have to talk about anything important, and you shouldn't talk about anything personal. Make a comment about how much rain we've had lately or about how long the line is for coffee today. Comment on someone's cool shoes or ask where he bought his backpack.

No matter what the topic, you need to speak. And the next time you see the same person, talk about something more substantive so you can eventually have a more meaningful conversation. Over time, you'll get to know and trust each other, which can lead to a relationship that's good for both of you.

Building trust starts with a simple "hello."

Still too shy to try it? Practice with a friend or make small talk with someone you already know.

BEHAVE

No matter how much a colleague or client likes you or wants to do business with you, that connection can shatter if you develop—or already have—a bad reputation.

In today's social media world, nothing you do in public is likely to remain private, so watch what you do and say.

In today's world of online reviews, nothing you say to or do with a client is likely to remain private either. So treat your clients with courtesy and make a good impression by doing a good job.

————————   ————————

I want people to be nice to me, so my aim is to be nice to everyone, all the time. The impression I give to everyone, I hope, is that I'm nice. I was raised in the South, where everyone's nice all the time. Southern hospitality is real, y'all.

My clients reward my niceness with referrals, references, and positive online reviews. I appreciate that, and I reward the vendors and service providers I deal with when I post positive online reviews about them.

I post a lot of online reviews, as a lot of people do. And I'm very honest about my experiences. I also read online reviews before I choose almost anything, from a restaurant to a doctor.

Not too long ago I posted a five-star review on Yelp while I was sitting in the waiting room of my new eye doctor. He hadn't even examined my eyes yet.

I met him briefly when I got to the office. He shook my hand and introduced himself. He told me to call him "Tim" instead of "doctor," and I told him to call me "Cindy." I mentioned his good reviews on Yelp, and he joked about how long it took him to write them all.

He was friendly, welcoming, and funny—not exactly what I would expect from an eye doctor or anyone in a busy doctor's office. I've been recommending him to everyone ever since.

That doctor isn't a salesperson, but he essentially convinced me to write a good online review and recommend him to my friends.

That's selling.

Be aware of how you're treating customers—and everyone else. So many people nowadays write online reviews, and they have an impact. A lot of people, like me, rely on them to help them decide which businesses to use and which ones to avoid.

The way the doctor handles his patients—and the way you handle your customers—is about sales, even though you're not a sales pro.

Professionals who know they do a good job never worry about online reviews.

One home remodeler I know actually encourages his clients to post online reviews. He stands by his quality work and is confident enough that they'll post good reviews that he sends each client an e-mail at the close of a job with links to Angie's List, Yelp, and other review sites.

A 2015 Google survey revealed that online reviews influence purchasing decisions more than 67 percent of the time—that means more than half of the people in the survey said online reviews are an important part of their decision making.

It used to be that when a customer had a bad experience, she would tell a few friends and family members—but now she can tell the whole world within a few minutes.

Be aware of your online presence, because it affects your reputation. And if your business doesn't have an online presence, be aware that it should. You're leaving business on the table if you don't have a website and an active social media presence.

Personal Brand

Working hard isn't the only way you build a good reputation. You have a personal brand as well. No matter how good your reputation—or how long it took you to build it—you can ruin it, along with your chances of success, in a heartbeat. If you post something unflattering online, it can spread quickly. If someone videotapes you behaving poorly, that can go online, too, and you can't stop it.

Police your own behavior, remarks, and social media posts with this in mind: Even private posts have a way of going public.

You never stop building your reputation, and it is your most valuable asset.

What kind of reputation have you built for yourself? Do people believe you are nice, dependable, honest, hard-working, fun? Do they view you as someone who will help out a friend or colleague whenever possible? Or do you have a reputation for lashing out, getting even, or berating your staff?

Your reputation is your decision. Your reputation is your personal brand.

A tip: Make yourself the kind of person others want to help. Make yourself the kind of person who makes it easy for clients, colleagues, bosses, and others to say "yes."

STEP THREE IN ACTION

———— OUTSELLING ————

You might not officially be in sales, but I'll bet there have been times when you thought you could do a better job than the sales pro who was supposed to be selling you.

I run into nonsalespeople all the time who outsell the pros, just because they're nice. Or because they listen. Or because they pay attention. Or because they care.

You know how your computer or smartphone always seems to crash when you can least afford to be without it? Like when you're racing against the clock to meet an important deadline? Or when you're planning a trip and you need to take the thing with you?

That's exactly what happened to me the afternoon before I had to fly from my home in San Francisco to New Orleans to give a speech at a conference of healthcare providers. Doctors are salespeople, too, after all.

It was 3:30 in the afternoon. I had just finished making my speech outline and planned to spend the rest of the day rehearsing. I would pack for the trip that evening, and then go to sleep early so I could get to the airport on time.

I hit "save." I exhaled. That's when I saw the dreaded blue screen of death.

My outline. My speech. My plans. My afternoon.

All gone in a second.

Luckily, I have a subscription to Best Buy Geek Squad, so I packed up my computer and dashed over there.

The tech at the counter told me it was probably the motherboard. Even if you're computer illiterate like I am, you know that's not a good thing to hear.

"No, no, no, no, no," I said to anyone and everyone.

I explained my dilemma to the tech. I didn't even care if he couldn't save the computer. I just needed my outline, a few other critical documents, and a new laptop.

Here's what the tech, who is not a salesperson, did: He paged a salesperson who works in the computer department, explained that I was in a hurry, and broke down exactly what I wanted: The same exact model as the one that had crashed. He said he would try to retrieve my outline while I purchased the laptop.

I can't tell you how much I appreciated this guy, but the salesperson absolutely blew it.

He started showing me a bunch of laptops and explaining the features of each one. I told him I didn't have time to shop, and that I was happy with my old laptop and simply wanted to replace it with the same model.

But he kept selling me, and I was annoyed.

So I said to him: "Hey, I know this is your job, but please stop pitching me. I'm in a hurry. I already know what I want."

I had to sell the salesperson on doing what I wanted. I wanted him to hurry up and let me buy the computer. Ironic, right?

I finally got the computer and brought it over to the tech guy, and I begged him to hurry. He quickly explained that if I bought a specific kind of warranty, it would allow him to move the frozen data from my broken computer onto my new one faster. He asked, "Do you want to buy the warranty?" I said, "Yes!"

I trusted him because he was listening to me. He understood what I needed and could see I was stressed and rushed. He was doing everything he could to give me what I needed.

It was after 4 p.m. His shift had ended at 4 p.m. He promised to stay until he solved my problem.

There was nothing I could do at the store, so I went home and packed.

And true to his word, the tech called me at 6:30 and told me to come on back. He had transferred all my data from the old computer to the new one. Not just my outline.

This tech's commitment to fixing my issue is what sold me. Not the salesperson, who did a terrible job, but the nonsalesperson, who turned a frantic moment into a solved problem. In the process, he created a customer for life.

———————   ———————

I've had a couple of similar experiences with nonsalespeople who have sold circles around the official sales reps.

My husband and I just finished remodeling our condo in San Francisco. If you've ever done a major renovation at home, you probably know that whatever can go wrong does go wrong.

Let me tell you a few stories.

I got a little bit overwhelmed when it was time to choose the granite for our kitchen countertops. So many choices!

As a result, I got behind on my shopping. The countertop installers were supposed to come in a week, and I hadn't chosen a slab yet. I needed to make a decision that day.

I had an appointment with a salesperson at the countertop store. When I got there, I was asked to wait for just a little while until the she finished up with another customer.

Another woman, in charge of coordinating deliveries between the store and the homeowners, overheard the request and approached me. She said, "Why don't you come with me? You don't have to wait. I'll help you."

I told her how overwhelming the countertop selection was for me.

She truly heard me.

She sat me down and asked me what kinds of colors and patterns I liked: light or dark, for example; bold or subtle.

Then she pulled samples from the showroom wall and showed me just two at a time. If I said I liked one, she asked me what I liked about it. If I didn't like it, she wanted to know why.

And she heard me.

That information gave her something to go on. The more pairs of tiles she showed me, the closer I got to something I might want to buy. I felt so comfortable with her. I no longer felt overwhelmed. I trusted her. You tend to trust people who take the time to really listen to you.

And then she actually said, "Will you trust me with something?"

"Absolutely."

She brought me back to the warehouse and pulled out a quartz slab.

I was there to buy granite, but the minute I saw the quartz, I wanted it.

The funny thing is, I had no idea what I wanted when I walked into that showroom. But this delivery coordinator, after spending just 20 minutes with me, seemed to know exactly what I wanted.

And she knew I wanted it today, so she didn't bother trying to sell me something that would have to be ordered. She knew what she had in inventory, and she knew exactly the piece that would suit me.

It did. She did. I bought it on the spot.

As if that weren't enough, she walked me to the cashier and asked the clerk to give me the 20 percent designer discount.

Sold!

For life. She's not even in sales.

Officially.

But unofficially, she knows she is.

I immediately wrote a glowing Yelp review for the company and this cool new friend. I told all the contractors who were working on my condo about her. I have recommended her to at least half a dozen friends and colleagues. And I know one of those friends has already bought from her and posted a rave on Yelp.

That's what can happen when someone who's not an official salesperson understands that every job is a sales job.

One more story about my remodeling project, and then I'll stop. If you've ever remodeled, you know the horror stories are endless.

Our condo is super-cozy, and by super-cozy, I mean it's really small. Most San Francisco condos are.

So we had to furnish it with smallish furniture.

This is a story about a pair of colleagues—one a sales pro and the other not—and the nonsalesperson who saved the day.

Just like you can.

I was looking for just the right chairs to go with the new table I bought for our compact dining room.

So we got to the furniture store, and I told the salesperson who met us at the door just what I was looking for. I showed her a chair in the showroom that I liked, but I wanted an upholstered seat instead of a hard, wood seat, and I wanted a shorter back in a specific wood finish. I showed her a picture. Simple, right?

I felt, right from the start, that she wasn't listening to me.

She started showing me a dozen wood samples, ranging from very dark to very light. But I had already decided on the wood. I had already said so.

Then she walked us over to the coffee tables and prattled on about all the sizes the store offers.

Annoying.

When she mentioned that the store offers free design services to its members, I asked how to become a member, and I joined on the spot.

At that moment, I would have done anything to get away from her.

I didn't buy that membership because she was a good salesperson; I bought it so I didn't have to deal with her. I wanted to talk to a designer who would listen to me.

And I got what I paid for.

The designer listened to my checklist for the chairs; she understood that size mattered. She asked a few questions, like whether I prefer a rustic or contemporary style. She said the store had multiple options of each in the wood finish I had preselected.

When I told her about my preference for a low-backed chair, she said that narrowed the selection considerably: The store sells only two models with low backs.

It was easy to choose between them; I liked one better right away.

Was that so hard?

The annoying salesperson was trying to upsell me because she wanted a bigger commission. The designer was trying to understand exactly what I wanted so she could get me exactly what I wanted.

In fact, when the salesperson circled back around a while later to check on me, I politely told her the designer was taking care of me now.

We bought four chairs for the table and two for the bedroom. The same day, we bought a bedroom suite and some accessory tables.

We bought all of that from the designer.

If we had stuck with the salesperson, we would have left the store empty-handed and utterly frustrated, I'm sure.

The designer was listening to me. The salesperson wasn't paying attention. She established zero trust with me. I felt like she was pushing me toward things I didn't want.

The designer listened. The designer got the commission. We got the furniture we wanted.

Even if you haven't had a day of sales training, you can sell circles around the pros if you listen to what the client, customer, colleague, boss, or friend is telling you she needs and wants.

Show her what you have that meets those needs. If you don't have anything, say so.

I've walked away from a gazillion sales because I don't have a product or service that will fill the needs of the person I am trying to sell.

And I've walked away from a gazillion salespeople who have tried to sell me products and services that will not fill my needs.

Sell people what they need, not what you need them to have or what you want them to do. You'll only know what they need if you listen.

Before my husband and I made our move back to the East Coast, we needed to store some of our furniture and equipment that we didn't want to haul across the country with us.

I shopped and shopped for a storage service, and I couldn't believe my luck when I found one that wouldn't make us haul our stuff to a storage locker and come and root through everything whenever we needed to take an item out.

Instead, Clutter came to our condo, packed up what we wanted to put into storage, and hauled it away. The company kept a detailed inventory and a photo of everything we stored, just in case we needed a random item at some point. When we moved back, the company brought all our stuff to our condo within 24 hours. The same guys who had hauled it away two years earlier took care of us this time, too.

After we got settled in, we realized that our skis had not been delivered to us. So I called the company. The person who answered the phone—sort of a traffic director for the lost-and-found department, but definitely not a salesperson—checked the inventory and didn't see any mention of skis.

What she did next made us customers for life.

I expected that the company would deny that it ever had our skis. It had no record of them.

I was prepared, and before that could happen, I pointed out that the company had stored our ski clothes, our helmets, and our poles. So it's pretty obvious that it had our skis.

But nobody denied it. Instead, the people at the company said they would look. And before they looked, they said they would pay us for the skis if they couldn't find them.

They established trust with us by truly hearing our side of the story. But my trust-o-meter raced to the highest level when they guaranteed that they would either find our skis or pay for them.

They never accused us of lying. They never doubted our word. They never denied having the skis. They never argued with us.

And then they found our skis. The guys had forgotten to list them on the inventory but had, in fact, put them in storage.

They wanted us to trust them, so they behaved in a trustworthy way.

We don't need a storage service anymore, but I have told every friend and colleague this story, and a few have hired the company, too. And you'd better believe that if we need storage again, our first and only call will be to Clutter.

My trust in the people there earned the company my referrals.

CHAPTER 7

—— STEP FOUR ——

Ask for What You Want

I'VE OBSERVED THAT ONE of the most difficult things for people to do is ask for what they want. Even if they really, really need it. Even if they absolutely deserve it. Even if they want it more than anything. Even if they sell for a living.

The straight truth is this: If you want something—anything—you're way more likely to get it if you ask for it than if you don't.

People can't read your mind. They don't know what you want unless you ask for it. Even if it seems obvious.

I know a real estate agent—or a former agent, I should say—who just couldn't bring himself to close a sale.

This guy was great at talking to people and getting their homes listed. He had lots of clients to show houses to, and they loved him, but he hardly ever sold a house. Why? Because he never came right out and asked his clients to buy one.

The agent was waiting for his clients to tell him they wanted to buy, but they rarely did. Instead, he just kept showing them house after house after house, and he never closed the deals because they were waiting for him to ask. As a result, he didn't make any money and is no longer a real estate agent.

——————— ———————

Do you ever notice how when we talk about getting a favor, or a raise, or a promotion, or a good deal, we use the word "ask"? We ask for a favor. We ask for a raise or a promotion. We ask for a discount.

The reason for this is that you have to ask for it or you just won't get it.

My observation from many years as a professional communicator, professor, consultant, and salesperson is that we don't ask for the things we want for three main reasons:

1. We're afraid we will be rejected.
2. We don't know exactly how to ask.
3. We don't think we deserve what we're asking for.

In this chapter, "Step Four: Ask for What You Want," I'll show you why it's so important to be willing to ask for the sale—or favor, or job, or promotion, or raise, or referral, or whatever it is you want. I'll suggest ways to overcome your fear and to muster up the courage to ask. And I'll give you a few helpful tips that might teach you how to ask in just the right way. Most importantly, I hope to show you that you really do deserve to have everything in life that you want and need.

FEAR

Most people are terrified of rejection—so much so that they would rather do without than ask someone who might say "no."

This was proved in a 2013 Stanford University study that found that most people automatically figure the answer to an ask will be "no." And that is even more evident if the person has said "no" to us in the past.

This study revealed something else, too: People who are asked tend to feel guilty about saying "no," especially if they have said "no" to you before.

It seems that our gut may be wrong when it comes to asking. You see, when we ask someone to give us a raise or a referral, or to do us a favor, all we think about is how much we're imposing on the other person. We're worried that the other person will feel put out or inconvenienced; that she won't have time to help us; or that it might cost her money to do what we're asking. We're afraid we're asking for too much, even if we're asking for something the person can reasonably do and might even happily do for us.

So instead we don't ask at all because we're too scared. Yet, at the same time, the person on the other end of the ask is worried, too. That person is afraid of what you might think of her if she says "no." She's worried you'll be mad or hurt or that you won't like her anymore. She's caught up in thinking about how awkward things will get if she says "no," and doesn't want to offend you.

Don't assume the answer will be "no." Expect a "yes" and see what happens!

I really do feel that most people really do want to help others, so go ahead and give them a chance to do so. Ask for their help and stop assigning motives to people before you even ask for what you want.

——————— ———————

One person I've been trying to convince that asking doesn't have to be so hard is my friend Patrick.

Patrick is a superstar at work. He comes in early, stays late, is focused on the job, has great ideas, and is a problem solver. He loves his job, his bosses love him, and he considers all his colleagues to be friends.

But he also knows that he would be getting paid at least one-third more if he worked at a competing company and suspects that other employees at his current company are earning more than he is.

Still, he won't ask for a raise—and he hasn't gotten more than the same cost-of-living raise as everyone else for the past five years.

That's because he believes that his boss knows how good he is and should offer him a raise because of it.

But I constantly explain to him that's not how things realistically work and follow up with the question: "Did your parents just raise your allowance every year when you were a kid? Or did you have to ask them to?"

He knows what he needs to do, but he won't ask. He is too afraid. And he won't hear a "yes" until he asks. It's a vicious cycle.

——————— ———————

My friend Donna is a freelance web designer with a master's degree and a long résumé of senior-level jobs with publishing houses. She tells a story about a potential client who called her with the offer of an interesting project. The client and Donna hit it off during the phone call, brainstormed about the project, and finally agreed to work together.

Then the client said, "This is a $25-an-hour job."

Donna, who typically charges $100 an hour, wasn't floored. It seems people routinely undervalue the work that designers do, mostly because people don't understand what it entails. In fact, Donna has fielded many calls from would-be clients offering even less; some offer as little as minimum wage. She turns them all down, of course.

This time, she had three choices: Say "yes," say "no," or negotiate something between $25 and $100.

She could have let fear rule her decision. She could have said "yes" to a fee that fell far short of what she usually charges just to ensure she didn't lose the job to another freelancer.

But she didn't. Instead she said, "I charge $100 an hour, but I can recommend another designer with less experience if you would like to hire someone for less money."

Donna was excited about the potential of landing such an interesting job, but not so much that she was willing to undervalue her skills and services. She explained the difference between what the client would get for $25 hour—in quality and speed, for instance—and what she could expect for $100. Donna handled the situation professionally in many ways—and because of that, the client agreed to the $100 fee and adjusted her expectations going forward.

Since this initial interaction, the pair have worked on several projects together over the years, and they both get what they want: Donna earns a fair wage, and the client gets service worth paying for.

Like Donna, you deserve to earn what you're worth. My advice: Speak up!

Settling

Here are three questions for you to answer the next time you decide to settle for what you have rather than ask for what you deserve. This exercise might help you if you're reluctant to ask for what you need at work, whether it's more money or responsibility, a seat on the board of directors, an additional team member for your project, or a new stapler to replace your broken one.

1. What do I have to gain versus what do I have to lose if I ask for what I want?

Are you truly putting your job—or anything else—on the line by asking for a raise? Of course not. What are you afraid of losing? Your job, your life, your friends, the boss's respect? Examine this honestly. How realistic is it to expect to lose something valuable just because you ask for something that you know you deserve?

On the other hand, what might you get? More money? A bigger office? Your own assistant? You'll never hear a "yes" until you ask for it.

Don't make your fear of rejection a self-fulfilling prophecy. How much respect do you think your boss or client has for someone who won't ask for what he's owed?

Focus on what you want and might get rather than on what you have to lose.

2. What is the absolute worst outcome?

Say you ask and the answer is "no." What is the most devastating imaginable consequence of that "no"?

It could be a little embarrassing or disappointing. It could mean that you'll have to consider looking for another job that will pay you more or treat you better. It could mean that you'll have to continue to work for less than you feel you're worth.

None of that is likely to make you happy. None of it means you're losing your job, though. None of it means you'll never be happy again. None of it means your colleagues will treat you any differently; unless you tell them, they'll never even know you asked. Your boss won't tell them.

Look at the worst-case scenario—which is so unlikely to happen anyway. But if it does, what does it really mean? How will that "no" change your life?

3. What will I do if I hear a "no"?

Be prepared for every objection that your boss might make when you ask for whatever it is that you need. Consider every scenario, and come up with an answer.

What if the boss says there's no money in the budget for a raise this year? What if he says the market is down?

Look at the entire situation. Take all those potential objections into account. Don't be afraid to keep asking. Have courage.

A "no" is probably temporary. A "no" often means "no for now," not "no forever."

COURAGE

No matter what you do in life, you'll do it better if you plan for it. Yes, we are back to planning. I truly can't overemphasize the value of planning because the more prepared you are, the more confident you will be. And the more confident you are, the less likely you are to get flustered, back down, or take "no" for an answer when you suspect a "yes" is not too far away.

I prepare for a big ask the same way I prepare for a big speech: by doing my research, both about the person I'm asking and about the thing I'm asking for.

For example, if I want a lawyer to do pro bono work for my favorite charity, I dig around a little to figure out if this particular lawyer has helped charities in the past, if he has a soft spot for this specific charity, if his firm has a quota of pro bono hours for each associate to fill, and so on. Then when we meet, I can talk about the project in the context of how offering free legal service would satisfy him: his quota, his desire to do community service, or his propensity for helping out those affected by the disease or condition that the recipients of this charity suffer from.

In short, I prepare myself so I will know how to create a win for the other person in a way that creates a win for me, too. This builds my confidence because I know I've done my homework and am likely to hear a "yes."

———— ————

Isabel is a former colleague of mine who made a plan in her early twenties to live in as many countries as possible during the course of her career. First up: France.

She had lived there for a semester in college, so she knew how to speak French. And after working one summer as a character at Walt Disney World in Florida, she decided to apply for a job at Disneyland Paris. She looked good for the job on paper, so someone from the resort's human resources department arranged to do a telephone interview with her—in French.

Isabel had one week to prepare. She started speaking French to everyone to brush up on her language skills. She prepared a list of bullet points to refer to during the interview so she wouldn't forget to tell the executive about her prior experience, her knowledge of Disney's characters and products, and her love of all things Disney. She looked at the interviewer's social media sites to learn what she could about her, and she bolstered her own social media to reflect her Disney connection.

She was nervous about the interview, but by the time her phone rang, she was ready for it. She was confident. She believed that once she told the interviewer about her skills as a performer, master of ceremonies, and speaker, Disneyland Paris would want to find a place for her among the resort's entertainers.

And that's exactly what Disneyland Paris did. She got the job there and kept it for three years before moving to Asia for her next career adventure.

Courage Boosters

If you want to approach your next ask with more courage, you need to make sure you have sufficient confidence in what you are asking for. Here are three ways to boost your chances for a "yes" and give you the courage to ask for one:

1. Ask the right person.

Too many times, we ask the wrong person. You'll never get a "yes" from a person who doesn't have the authority to give you one. And if you do, it won't be an authentic "yes" that you can follow up on.

Don't make the mistake of thinking that anyone in authority at a business can say "yes" to your request. Pitching your great marketing idea to the vice president of finance isn't likely to get you very far.

2. Make it personal.

You know yourself and your motives better than anyone else. You can feel confident about your ask if you can make it personal.

To do that, explain why you're asking. When someone understands why something is important to you, she might be more likely to agree to do it.

This is the premise of the book *Start with Why: How Great Leaders Inspire Everyone to Take Action*, by the ever-optimistic Simon Sinek. His advice: It's just as important to understand why you're doing something as it is to know what you're doing.

That's true when you're asking someone for help—or a raise or a referral or anything. If the person understands why you're asking, he is more likely to say "yes." If the person understands what he'll get out of the deal, he is more likely to say "yes."

So explain how a "yes" can help both him and you. A few tips:

- Share the reason why you want the person to do what you ask. Describe the downside to your colleague of not saying "yes."

- Couch your conversation in a way that shows the other person how he can benefit from helping you. Nine times out of ten, it works.
- Offer to help him with his part.
- If he asks for your help, pitch in. Make good on your offer.

3. Have pure motives.

I'm not kidding when I tell you that every sale I make is one that benefits the person who's "buying."

To me, sales (even unofficial sales like we're talking about here) are an opportunity to help someone, make someone's life easier, or solve another person's problem. If what I have to offer—a product, a service, or an idea—can in some way ease someone's burden, that's what I sell.

But if I don't have anything like that to offer, I don't pretend that I do.

If I ask someone to leave his regular vendor and bring his company's business to me, I know that I can offer him a better deal, or more attention, or another benefit if he does.

If I ask a client to refer my company to his associates so they will bring their business to me, I promise and deliver the excellent and respectful service that will make my client look good for recommending me.

My motives are always pure.

WORDS

How you ask for something can be just important as *what* you ask for.

The most important thing to remember when you ask someone for anything is that you are asking, not demanding or telling the other person to do it.

It's important to be confident and to expect a "yes."

I've seen too many people fail at the ask because they chose the wrong words. They were requiring, not requesting.

Don't be that person. Instead, vow to never make the following mistakes.

1. The Demand

Beth is a single parent who works two jobs, both on weekdays. She works as an office manager during the day, and after that, she works at a veterinary clinic. She works at the clinic from 5:30 until 8 p.m., until the overnight pet-sitter arrives to relieve her. Then she rushes home to spend one precious hour with her daughter before bedtime.

But for the past couple of months the overnight caretaker at the vet, Trina, has been arriving late, sometimes by as much as half an hour. So Beth tried to sell her on getting to work on time. She tried three different tactics:

First, "You need to start getting here on time. I have to be home by 8:30." That didn't work.

Second, "Trina: I told you I have to leave on time every night so I can see my daughter before she goes to bed. Please get here on time." That didn't work, either.

That's when things clicked for Beth. She wasn't selling, asking, or persuading.

She was demanding—and demanding isn't selling. Demanding is not a way to convince someone that giving you what you want will be good for both of you.

When you want something, ask for it—but only after figuring out what the other person will get out of saying "yes."

Finally, Beth realized that she needed to find out why Trina, who used to arrive at work on time, has been late every day lately. So she tried for the third time.

She asked: "Hey, Trina, is everything OK at home? I noticed that you're coming in a little later."

Instead of acting angry and demanding, Beth is concerned and interested. And she really is, because Trina is her coworker and Beth cares about her.

It turns out that Trina is having her own childcare issues. She has chosen her shifts so she only works on the evenings when her son sleeps at his father's house. For the past couple of months, the father has been unreliable about picking the kid up on his nights, and Trina winds up frantically calling neighbors and relatives to find someone to watch the boy. It makes her late.

Now Beth knows what Trina needs, and the two brainstorm ideas to try to come up with a solution to both of their problems.

In this scenario, Beth asked questions that helped her understand what Trina needed. Once the two of them understood each other, they were better able to help each other.

Like so many of us, Beth was thinking only of her needs, but you won't get very far with a sale—or in life, for that matter—if you don't pay attention to the needs of the people around you.

2. The Out

Carmen, a photographer, takes a completely different approach when she asks for what she wants. She'll say something like: "Can you show me how to save this file to the new network? You don't have to if you're too busy. I'll try to figure it out. I can probably figure it out."

Carmen's word choice conveys the message that she is lazy and hasn't tried to solve this problem on her own. Instead, she's looking for the other person to solve her problems for her. Yet, the reality is that Carmen can't figure it out. She's very smart and already tried on her own. Asking for help is her last resort.

Carmen's best approach is first to figure out what the other person will get in return for helping her and then to say something like this: "Hey, would you mind showing me how to do this? I want to make it easy for you to find these photos on the new network when you need them."

She's asking someone to help her help him in the long term.

Win-win.

135

3. The Awkward Silence

Juan works for a polling company, where his job is to ask people to give him information. Yet, very few people actually give him what he asks for, most likely because of how he asks: "I'm calling to ask you about the upcoming election. Do you plan to vote for Candidate A or Candidate B?"

Every time the person on the other end pauses, Juan fills the silence immediately and says, "If you don't want to tell me, that's OK." Or sometimes he says, "If that's too personal, you don't have to answer."

Juan fails to consider that the person on the other end might need a minute to think, may support the opposite candidate, or has been interrupted from another task because she answered the phone.

Juan needs to realize that he's asking someone else to give information—and he needs to be patient enough to give the person a minute to decide how to respond. If he doesn't, he won't last in that job.

He needs to learn that silence is OK. Wait for the other person to answer. Give people time to think. Consider the fact that the person might be undecided and need to take a minute.

You don't need to fill the void.

Consider the awkward silence a game of chicken. Whoever speaks first loses.

4. The Open-Ended Invitation

Raj and Anita work in similar jobs at different companies and met when they sat at the same table at a city planning meeting luncheon. They hit it off immediately.

In his job, Raj was responsible for coming up with the arguments that would convince state, county, and city governments to make exceptions to zoning laws when a corporation wanted to build its headquarters someplace where large buildings weren't allowed. Anita worked with those same governments to encourage them to grant tax incentives to similar companies as a reward for all the new jobs they would offer to the locals.

As they chatted about their projects, Raj realized and vocalized to Anita that she had access to the very database that he needed to sell a local city council on a firm he represented. When lunch was over, Raj handed Anita his card and said, "You can call me about the database."

Anita never called.

Raj missed the sale because he didn't ask for it. All he had to do was hand Anita his card and ask, "Would it be OK if I called you on Monday to talk more about the database?"

You can avoid these open-ended invitations by directly asking the other person to help you. Remember, it's your job to ask for what you want and your job to follow up.

5. The One and Done

Eliza is the executive assistant to the CEO of a company that arranges events featuring high-profile newsmakers like politicians, athletes, and Nobel Prize winners. The people who are invited to the events pay an annual membership fee just to be invited. They buy tickets to the events.

The CEO likes the room to be full at these events, especially for the most prominent speakers. So part of Eliza's job is to follow up on the formal, mailed invitations that the firm sends by calling the members personally to let them know about the events in case they want to buy tickets.

She's great at it—as long as nobody answers the phone. Eliza is the queen of voice mail. Her messages are eloquent, well stated, to the point, and helpful to anyone who wants to call back for a ticket or buy one online.

But Eliza, who considers herself a manager, planner, and organizer, doesn't think of those reminder calls as sales, so she never follows up to ask for the sale. As a result, she makes very few sales.

Giving someone information, including instructions for how to buy something, isn't the same as asking someone to buy something.

Eliza leaves a voice mail and crosses that client off her list. What she should do instead is leave a voice mail message and then call again a couple of days later to try to reach the person so she can ask for the sale again personally.

Without follow-up, you'll lose most of your unofficial sales.

THE ASK FORMULA

When it's time for me to come right out and ask for a sale, I follow a simple formula that might work for you, too:

1. Introduce yourself.

Nine times out of ten, your opportunities to make unofficial sales will be with someone you already know. But if you're pitching to someone you don't know, give your name.

Put yourself into context: "Hi, I'm Dr. Cindy McGovern. We met at the Black-and-White Gala in March, and I thought of you today because I remember you said you really like so-and-so. I wanted to let you know about an event." Or "My name is Cindy McGovern. I'm in your airline's frequent flyer club, and I'm hoping you can help me with something." Or "I'm Dr. Cindy. My friend Mark said you might be willing to talk to me about how to find a literary agent."

2. Put the other person in an empowering position.

After introducing yourself, kindly acknowledge something about the other person in order to make him or her more likely to at least listen to your pitch. Is she wearing the most gorgeous brooch you've ever seen? Tell her. Do you love the suit he's wearing? Say it. A little compliment—as long as it's authentic—can go a long way toward predisposing someone to say "yes."

And it doesn't always have to be a compliment. Instead, this is something you do with the end goal of empowering the other person.

Here's an example:

My friend Greg travels an awful lot for work and rents his fair share of cars. He is a master of making people feel empowered before he asks for a rental car upgrade.

He'll say, "What kind of car did *they* put me in today?" The agent will tell him.

Then Greg will say, "What can *you* put me in?"

He says weary travelers rarely take the time to notice the agents who check them in. He does. He puts them in a power position. He acknowledges that they are in positions of authority and can make decisions. He asks them to make a decision on his behalf.

That might make the day of someone whom so many people treat as invisible. Getting that compliment might be all the incentive the agent needs to give Greg something in return.

3. Offer your help.

Even though you're the one who is asking for something, it's important to offer something in return, too. If you listen carefully enough, you'll hear what the other person wants or needs, and you shouldn't be afraid to offer a solution.

For example, a customer who came to you for one service might reveal a problem that you could solve by selling her a completely different service. If she buys it, you both get what you want.

If you have a solution that can fill the other person's need, focus on that—not on what you'll get.

If you're pitching someone you just met, follow the guidelines in Chapter 6 ("Step Three: Establish Trust") to listen, observe, talk, and establish trust until you understand just how you might be able to help someone by putting him together with something your company has to offer. Then use that language to make the sale: "My company has a service that I know can help you solve your problem. Would you like to sign up for it?"

4. Ask for what you want.

As we've seen throughout this chapter, asking for what you want is the hard part, but finding the words to actually ask someone for something is easier when you come from a place of genuine helpfulness.

"Can I help you with that by offering you this service?"

"Would you like to try this out?"

"Would you do us the honor of speaking at our annual meeting?"

And finding the right words is easier when you come from a place of gratitude. Even though you haven't made the sale yet, consider how much you will appreciate this person if she says "yes." Choose your words with that in mind:

"Would you be willing to help me?"

"Could I ask you for a favor? I could really use your help."

"I will be so grateful if you could do this for me."

Nonsalespeople and even some of the sales professionals I work with constantly ask me to give them a script for how to ask for the sale. I say "no," because a genuine ask isn't scripted. It's the conclusion of a dialogue.

Putting It All Together

With these four tips in mind, here's what a successful ask might sound like:

"Hi Nikko! I'm Dr. Cindy McGovern. Do you remember meeting me in Chicago last month at the bar association convention? I really enjoyed that convention. Did you have a good time?

"I won't keep you too long, Nikko. I just remember that you seemed like you were so willing to help out your colleagues—which I remembered because I'm that way, too. I was wondering if you might be willing to help me out? I'm hoping you wouldn't mind introducing me to your vice president of marketing . . ."

PRO TIP

Make every transaction a human interaction. And don't forget that everyone you deal with is a human, so you should speak to people the way you would like them to speak to you.

PERMISSION

One revealing reason why so many people do not ask for what they want and need is because they don't believe they deserve to have it. So they settle for what they already have or for what's offered to them. They say "OK" when they are secretly screaming for something more or something extra.

I don't settle. I ask for what I want. And while I can't say I get it 100 percent of the time, I get it most of the time. I deserve to. And so do you. And I know I might not get what I deserve if I don't ask for it.

What do you deserve? To be a classroom assistant when you're just as qualified to teach the entire class yourself? To earn less than another employee who has the exact same job—and the courage to ask for more money? What are you willing to do to get what you deserve?

Are you willing to ask for it?

Study after study says people are not. Women, especially, are not willing to ask for what they want.

When economics professor Linda Babcock asked her dean why male graduate students at her college tended to be lead instructors and female students were assigned as assistants, the answer was simple: "More men ask."

Same goes for men who negotiate higher salaries: They're more likely to ask, so they're likely to earn more.

In her book *Women Don't Ask: Negotiation and the Gender Divide*, Babcock and her coauthor, writer Sara Laschever, explain that some women don't even realize they're allowed to ask for more than they're offered. Others are afraid to ask because they fear they might not get the job if they ask for more money. Or they imagine they could damage a relationship with a coworker or boss if they're bold enough to ask for what they want and deserve. Or they have learned that society sometimes punishes women who speak up about what they want and need.

For many, asking seems like an act that's too bold. Asking implies that you deserve something that you don't have, and to some, that might seem conceited or selfish or even greedy.

But is it?

Is there some reason why we can't ask for what we want and have what we want?

Why would it be considered egomaniacal for someone to say, "I deserve it"?

You do deserve it. But as we learned from my friend Patrick and the real estate agent from the beginning of this chapter, knowing that you deserve more isn't going to get you any more. You have to ask.

Dig deep and try to figure out why you believe you don't deserve to have what you want. At least not strongly enough to ask for it.

If you didn't know you are allowed to ask, please let me be the one to clue you in: You're allowed to ask. And while I advise people to make requests that are reasonable, you're even allowed to ask for way more than you think anyone would ever give you.

Still, an examination of what you believe you truly deserve can lead you to some painful truths.

You might, for instance, realize that you're steaming over not getting something that you really didn't earn. So while you're convincing yourself that you deserve what you're asking for—and please practice that every day—make sure you're not insisting on something that you actually do not deserve.

Be honest. Did you earn it? Or did you knock yourself out of the running by doing something you shouldn't have? Are you reluctant to ask because you don't believe you deserve it? Or because you know you don't?

I'm still saying that you should ask for everything you believe you deserve. But as I said above, be honest with yourself: Do you deserve it? Once you recognize the difference between what you truly deserve and what you haven't earned, it will be easier to ask for what you want and need.

But the "yes" isn't automatic. Even if you truly deserve what you're asking for, you might have to prove that you really want it and deserve it.

Ask with confidence. The fact is that we teach people how to treat us. If we don't believe we deserve as much money as others in the same job, others won't believe it, either. If we don't believe we deserve the things we want, we don't ask for them. If you're not asking, examine your beliefs at their root. You can't convince others if you can't convince yourself.

STEP FOUR IN ACTION

———— THE "ICK" FACTOR ————

If you've ever been to a mall during the Christmas shopping season, you've experienced what I like to call the "ick" factor.

It's that slimy, used feeling you get after you've spent way too much money at a kiosk on a bunch of products that you definitely don't need but that a handsome, fast-talking young man with a charming accent has talked you into before you even knew you were being hoodwinked.

It's the anger you seethe with when you get your bill for $15,000 or $25,000 for the time-share you bought on impulse after listening to a high-pressure sales pitch for a vacation plan that you really would love to own but can't afford. But it's too late because you've already signed the papers.

It's the dread that engulfs you after you hire a couple of guys in a pickup truck to replace your roof shingles with discounted materials left over from a job they did for your neighbor a few blocks over—and they disappear with your deposit, never to return.

So when I tell you that every job is a sales job and encourage you to sell, I'm not one bit surprised when your response is, plain and simple, "Ick."

Some of the people who sell this way are professional salespeople, and others are just plain crooks. But collectively, they have made a lot of us distrustful of all salespeople and given the profession a big black eye.

I want to pause here and tell you that I've worked with thousands of sales professionals, and I can assure you that the majority of them are honest and aboveboard and represent legitimate products and services.

I also want to say I know that's hard for you to believe, especially if you have been victimized by an unscrupulous salesperson—fake or legit. But that doesn't mean you have to sell that way. I don't sell that way, not ever. Instead, when I ask someone for something—for anything—I consider it a request. A proposal. Something I hope for. I don't demand. I don't assume. I don't pressure. I don't bully. I don't insist. I don't bribe. And I don't threaten. I'm polite, conversational, accommodating, and absolutely as helpful as I can possibly be when I ask.

I don't do "ick."

In fact, most sales professionals embrace a code of ethics that requires those in sales to avoid doing anyone any harm; follow the law; deal in good faith; build relationships; and treat people with honesty, responsibility, fairness, respect, and transparency.

I abide by this code, and I go further. I follow a code my grandma taught me when I was way too young to know what the word "sell" meant: Treat others the way you would like them to treat you.

I like to be treated with kindness, so I treat others with kindness.

So when I sell, I'm nice. I don't push or pressure. And I never try to sell people something that they don't need or that they'll regret buying.

My brand of sales is to sell people what they need. I sell them solutions to problems. I don't sell them at all if I don't have anything that they need or want.

In that case, I walk away empty-handed. That's OK with me. I'd rather keep my ethics than make a sale.

I get the sale only if I give something worthwhile in return.

I used to think sales were icky, cheesy, and borderline immoral, too. Then I started learning more about selling. Once I did, I realized it's not selling that's icky. It's those few unscrupulous salespeople who are.

So I detached myself from them in every way, shape, and form. I don't act like them. I don't sell like them. I don't associate with them. I don't take them on as clients. I don't partner with them on projects.

My brand of selling is about creating relationships. I believe I make my living by helping people. I don't see how I could be in any other job. Helping is what I'm good at. Helping is what I like to do. Helpful is in my nature and personality.

I'm a *helpaholic* so much so that I actually own the trademark on the word. Maybe you are, too. If so, embrace selling as a form of helping, and maybe, just maybe, the "ick" factor will disappear.

If you can embrace selling as a form of helping, you won't behave like those creeps who bait-and-switch or lie or pressure you into spending money you don't have.

That's harm, not help. My brand of selling is to help. And my reputation is that I'm helpful. When clients refer me to others, they say I helped them. They never say I "sold" them.

You can make "helpful" what you do for a living, too. It will help you in return.

CHAPTER 8

— STEP FIVE —

Follow Up

EVERY FALL, A COUPLE of weeks before Thanksgiving, I stay home from work, turn off my phone, and sit at my dining room table all day. Hour after hour, I write personal thank you notes to everyone who has helped me along the way: family, teachers, mentors, old classmates, friends, clients, vendors, bosses, and colleagues.

I enclose each thank you into a beautiful Thanksgiving-themed greeting card. I pause after I finish each one, just to absorb what I've written and keep a thought about the person I wrote it to.

Some of the cards go to people I haven't seen or heard from in years—but they hear from me, every year.

I take the "thanks" in Thanksgiving seriously. If there's one thing I know for sure, I didn't get where I am on my own—and neither did you. All those friends and coworkers who supported me, taught me stuff, listened to my gripes, and held my hand through my heartbreaks and disappointments over the years contributed to this very happy life I live now.

I'm grateful, and I tell them. Every year.

PRO TIP

Say thank you in writing. Text, e-mail, and phone calls are nice, but nothing says, "I have time for you" louder than a handwritten note.

I call the final step in my five-step sales process "Follow Up," but I could call it "Gratitude."

I am authentically grateful to the barista at my favorite coffee shop who brightens each morning of my weekday by smiling and joking around, even when there's a never-ending line of bleary-eyed, caffeine-starved customers pressing him to work faster. I'm thankful for a client I had 10 years ago who continues to recommend my consulting firm to his colleagues. I'm still grateful for the grad school professor who wrote me the beautiful recommendation letter that helped me land my first job in academia.

I appreciate you for reading this book. I appreciate you for taking the time to explore this scary world of sales. I appreciate you for choosing my book over all the others you considered. And I want to thank you in advance for buying the books I will write in the future.

Nobody does this life alone. If you feel grateful, say it out loud. Mail a letter. Write a note. Send some flowers.

Shake a hand. Give a hug. Nod and smile. Whatever's your style. But get it done.

We all appreciate a little gratitude, whether we're giving it or receiving it.

So when you make one of the unofficial sales we've been examining in this book, don't just jump for joy on the inside. Put it out there. Say "thank you." Return the favor. Offer a compliment. Nominate someone for an award. Pay it forward.

A casual sales transaction typically ends in one of three ways: yes, no, or maybe.

Everybody wants the "yes." But as I outlined in this book, that can take planning, strategy, patience, kindness, and understanding. Do all that, and, unfortunately, sometimes you'll still hear a "no."

Say "thank you" anyway.

Making a sale, you know by now, isn't just about you or about what you can get right now. It's about agreements between two people who both benefit from the transaction—now or in the future.

When you give something, you get something. Whenever you get something, your authentic gratitude will not only let the other person know you appreciate him or her; it also will help you realize how much you depend on others and they depend on you. It's an awesome and humbling feeling.

This step, "Follow Up," will help you understand that your reaction to any response—yes, no, or maybe—can predict future results the next time you ask someone for something.

This chapter will teach you how to respond, whether it's a yes, a no, or a maybe. And throughout this section, you will hear me say again and again: Be grateful. Feel grateful. Show your gratitude.

Nobody does this alone.

YES

"Yes" is what you want to hear when you are asking a client for a referral, suggesting that a customer or a colleague do future business with you, asking a vendor for a discount, or pitching a proposal. But so many people don't know how to accept that "yes" for what it is, and here's what it is: It's a "Yes, you can have what you asked for."

So when you hear "yes," stop selling. Start showing gratitude.

Another author I know was a little bit embarrassed when she learned this lesson.

She had already pitched an idea for her second book to a publisher, and she was in a meeting with him and the woman who would become her editor for the project. They were negotiating her fee.

My friend felt she had undersold herself when she agreed to a fee for her first book a few years earlier. That was her first time, and she probably didn't have the confidence she has now. So this time, she asked the publisher and editor to increase her fee by approximately one-quarter.

The publisher seemed OK with her ask, but the editor wasn't. The editor said this book would be easier to write because my friend already had the first one under her belt.

My friend explained that she had undersold herself the first time. She didn't say so, but she was ready to walk away from the table if she didn't get the fee increase. The publisher must have sensed that.

He agreed to her terms, and he said "yes."

But my friend kept on selling. She explained her long experience in the field she wrote about, the lack of editing her first book needed, and so on.

Then the publisher asked a question: "Did you get what you wanted?"

"I did," my friend said.

"Then stop selling us," replied the publisher.

Embarrassed, my friend shut up.

Once you get what you want, accept it, say thanks, stop selling, and start planning for the next step.

My friend got what she wanted, and "thank you" was all she needed to say.

Now that we've worked so hard to get to that "yes," it's time we learned the proper way to respond when we get that coveted response.

It won't surprise you that my starting point is to be grateful.

Where I'm from, people say "thank you" all the time. I thanked the sales manager who charged me double for an order of copier paper once he refunded my money. I even said "thank you" to the little rascal who stole the box that Amazon left for me at my front door when his mother brought him over to return it.

No matter where you're from, somebody taught you to say "thank you" whenever someone gives you a gift.

A "yes" to your request for a favor, a raise, a job, a recommendation, or a second chance is a gift, so you should say "thank you" accordingly.

But true gratitude is more than words. I like to say that "gratitude" is a verb and that you should show and live your gratitude. You should be and act grateful.

Here are just a few ways to show your gratitude when you receive a "yes":

- **Return the favor.** Did someone refer a client to your company because you asked for a referral? Refer a client to his company next time you meet someone your firm can't help but the other guy's business can.
- **Say "yes" in return.** Next time a helpful colleague, client, or acquaintance asks you for a professional favor, agree to it if you can.
- **Send an e-mail.** Do it the minute you get back to your office after having a conversation with someone who agreed to help you. Make it genuine, even if it is digital.
- **Write a thank you letter—by hand.** Mail it. That makes it extra special. Write something personal. Express your heartfelt thanks. Say why

you're grateful. Explain how much the person has helped you.

- **Give a gift.** Just a token. I like to buy $10 gift cards from Starbucks or Amazon to enclose in some thank you cards. Sometimes I wait until the holidays to hand them out, and sometimes I offer them up the day after I hear the "yes."
- **Send flowers.** How delighted are you when you're surprised at the office by a delivery of colorful tulips or daffodils? That's how happy you can make someone else feel when you send flowers to her.
- **Post a review on the web page of the company where the person works.** Name the person. Say what she did for you.
- **Post reviews on Yelp and other customer review sites.** Say how great the person who helped you is and how much you enjoyed doing business with that person's company.
- **Update the person.** When someone does something for you, she naturally would like to know how it all worked out. Let her know.
- **Keep in touch.** The most genuine form of gratitude is an offer of ongoing friendship. It shows the other person that you weren't being nice just so you could get something. It shows him that you're not finished with the relationship just because you got what you wanted. It also makes it more likely that this acquaintance will remember you when the opportunity for a referral or a future unofficial sale presents itself.

"Thank you" shouldn't mean "goodbye." Instead, to me it means, "I'm so grateful for what you've done for me, and I'm looking forward to many more meetings, transactions, and communications in the future."

To me, gratitude is forever. If you get a "yes" from a person whom you have no way to stay in touch with, then pay it forward, which is a true sign of gratitude as well.

Here's an example of what can happen when we treat a "sale" as a one-off.

My friend Amanda got to know a local massage therapist pretty well when she started seeing her on a monthly basis after she hurt her back.

During Amanda's first appointment with Lynette, the women hit it off, and from then on, they talked nonstop during every hour Lynette spent working on Amanda's sore muscles.

Eventually, they started inviting each other to parties at their homes. They introduced each other to their families. They even occasionally met for happy hours.

Lynette was self-employed, so she decided to pick up some extra income on the side by selling high-end pots and pans. To get started, she asked her friends if she could pitch the cookware to them. Amanda and her husband said yes.

The company she represented had a business model that required the part-time salespeople to visit the potential client's home and use the scratch-resistant, stick-free pots and pans to cook dinner. So Lynette went to Amanda's and made dinner.

The couple probably would not have bought the set—which cost more than $1,000 for just a few pieces—if the salesperson hadn't been Amanda's friend. But both husband and wife were happy to help Lynette get her side business started.

As part of the deal, Amanda was entitled to invitations to monthly cooking lessons that featured additional pieces as door prizes and promised a free stainless-steel bowl guaranteed to keep food hot or cold.

When no invitations came, Amanda called Lynette to ask about the cooking lessons and her free bowl. Lynette became vague and even seemed to be avoiding Amanda. Eventually, Lynette secured the invitation for Amanda and arranged to meet her at the lesson with the free bowl.

Amanda went to the lesson, but Lynette never showed up. Amanda never got her bowl.

And for some reason—Amanda still doesn't know why—Lynette stopped responding to Amanda's voice mails. And Amanda never got invitations to future cooking lessons.

Amanda felt used. It seems Lynette got what she wanted from Amanda and didn't need anything else.

"Thank you" in this case meant "goodbye."

And no surprise here: Amanda stopped booking massage appointments with Lynette because she was so offended. The two never saw each other again.

In the sales biz, we know a proper thank you can create a customer for life. And we call what Lynette did to Amanda the "pitch and ditch."

You don't have to be a sales pro to know that if you treat people like they mean nothing more to you than their checkbooks, you will constantly be selling to strangers—because none of your prior customers will ever say "yes" again.

That's like going only on first dates. Every date is awkward, and you never really get to know anyone.

Sure, your goal is to make a sale—official or unofficial. But your overriding objective should be to build ongoing relationships with the people who were nice enough to help you out. They just might be nice enough to say "yes" again and again.

More important than anything on the list above, though, is making sure you deliver what you promised when you made your "sale."

If you sold a product, follow up with the customer to make sure it's operating well and filling the need you promised it would.

If you won approval for a project by convincing the boss you would do stellar work, then do stellar work.

If you got someone to refer you or your company to another business, treat that new business like it's gold. Not only is your reputation on the line, but so is the reputation of the person who referred you.

———————   ———————

One final note about the "yes": Consider it an invitation to ask for something else.

As we discussed in Chapter 7 ("Step Four: Ask for What You Want"), you have to be bold enough to ask for what you want, need, and deserve. Once you ask and hear a "yes," you are very likely to hear a "yes" from that person again and again. Especially if you show your sincere gratitude, keep in touch, and return the favor when that person calls on you for help.

We tend to say "yes" to people we like, when we feel good about doing the favor we're asked to do, or when doing it will get us something in return, like a solution to a problem.

Leverage those good feelings and turn that "yes" into more of them. The best way to do that—and the most important ask you can make—is to request that the person refer you to her colleagues, friends, family, and others. Strangers are more likely to say "yes" when someone they already know and trust says they can trust you, too. And referrals can open doors to you that otherwise might slam shut in your face.

If you keep your promises, are grateful and act like you are, and keep in touch with the people who say "yes," you will earn those referrals. And those referrals are so very important to the future of your business. Yet most of us seem as afraid to ask for a referral as we are to ask for a raise.

Remember, sales are not automatic, and most people don't even think about sending other helpful people your way, so if you don't ask for them, that's the same as leaving money on the table.

NO

Rejection stings everyone, even the most seasoned sales-person. So for someone like you, who doesn't formally sell for a living, that "no" can be especially disheartening. Still, as we discussed in "Step Four: Ask for What You Want," you'll live through it.

Most of the time, rejection isn't really personal. I've heard "no" a gazillion times. It doesn't stop me from asking for a "yes" the next time and the time after that.

I also understand that the answer is automatically "no" if I don't even ask. I can't possibly hear a "yes" if I don't try. So I take the risk, and now I hear "yes" more often than I hear "no." And when I do hear a "no," I don't let it get in the way of my success.

Sometimes, you just have to take "no" for an answer. But that doesn't mean the sale is necessarily lost.

I'm not a fan of aggressive time-share sales reps, but I heard a story about one sales pro that sort of impressed me.

I have a friend who owns a time-share with Hilton Grand Vacations and can take vacations all over the world. She loves the arrangement, and in just five or six years, she has paid a hefty fee to upgrade her owner-ship twice so she can use the time-share for more weeks each year.

Every summer, she and her husband take a morning out of their beach vacation to sit through a sales pitch designed to sell them even more time. They do it in exchange for hotel bonus points. They leave exhausted and feeling like the time-share company really couldn't care less if they were to go into debt, which would mar the good experience they've had so far with their vacations.

But last summer, they explained to the sales rep that even though they would love to buy more time, they were just there for the bonus points. They said they had to pay $20,000 to put a new roof on their home that fall, so there was no way they could afford to upgrade again this year. Then the rep did something unexpected. She spent the rest of the required hour coaching them about how to use their hotel bonus points to extend the time they could vacation—without upgrading.

She helped them figure out how they could accumulate enough bonus points—by signing up for the hotel chain's credit card and by using that card whenever they stayed in a hotel—to spend their twenty-fifth wedding anniversary in Venice next year, for free, in one of that chain's hotels.

The couple left the meeting exhilarated rather than exhausted, and the wife saved the rep's card so when they are ready to upgrade again, they can do it through this rep so she will be the one to earn the commission.

That rep heard "no" but listened to why. Instead of insisting and badgering and trying to wear the couple down, she realized that she really wasn't going to make a sale that day. Instead of giving up on the couple, treating them poorly, or shooing them away, she made what I call a "sale for tomorrow."

She laid the groundwork for that future upgrade by impressing the couple rather than upsetting them, as prior sales reps had done, and she sold them a credit card, and she sold them on using it instead of a different one whenever they traveled.

"No" doesn't always mean "no forever" or "no to everything." Instead, it could mean "no to this" but "yes to that." "No" doesn't always mean "no chance."

The time-share rep turned a hard "no" into a "yes" to a credit card and a "maybe next year" for the upgrade, which was not what she was going for, but was still a pretty great outcome.

My advice when you hear a "no":

- **Be helpful.** Remember that you won't get if you don't give.
- **Never whine.** Instead, acknowledge and own the problem. Offer a better deal.
- **Don't get mad when you hear a "no."** Anger, disrespect, blame, and badgering have never turned a "no" into a "yes."
- **Be gracious in defeat.** You never know when someone who said "no" will change her mind and decide to give you a call. You never know when someone said "no" because what you were offering him wasn't right for his company—but he knows someone whose company it's perfect for and is willing to tell him about you.

———————   ———————

You never know when a "no" means that a "yes" is right around the corner, maybe in a form you didn't expect.

So when you hear a "no," be just as nice and thankful as you are when you hear a "yes." Keep in touch with the person who said "no." Ask for something else a few months later. Tell people good things about that person. Keep him in mind for opportunities that cross your desk.

The fact is, most of the time, a "no" isn't personal. It's not about you. It's not a reflection on whether you're worth saying "yes" to. Most of the time, you get a "no" because the other person isn't interested in what you're offering. Or he can't afford it. Or it's not a good time. Or he's not authorized to say "yes."

Do what that time-share agent did: Listen to why the person is saying "no." Then see if you've got something he or she does want—now or later.

Another tip for how to handle a "no" is not to appear desperate. The best way to avoid that is not to get yourself into a desperate situation. Don't promise your boss that you can absolutely deliver something that depends on someone else's "yes." You can't control what that other person will say or do. So don't put all your eggs in one basket if you really need a "yes." Be prepared to ask more than one person.

I like to think of every "no" as a "no for now."

The smartest thing you can do when you hear a "no" that seems like it might really be a "not sure" is to find out why the person you've asked to help you is turning you down. So ask questions and really listen to the answers.

MAYBE

A scene from the 1994 Jim Carrey comedy *Dumb and Dumber* always makes me laugh. Carrey's character has just asked his love interest what the chances are that the two of them might end up together.

"Not good," she admits.

"You mean 'not good,' like one out of 100?" Carrey asks.

"I'd say more like one out of a million," she clarifies.

His response: "So you're telling me there's a chance? Yeah!"

Like Carrey's character, we often mistake "maybe" as a "yes." The reality is, "maybe" almost always means "no"; that's why I call it the "slow no."

Same goes for "I'll try," and "I'll do my best," and "I'll see."

Remember when your parents used to give you answers like that when you were a kid?

You'd ask, "Can I have this toy?"

And they would answer, "Maybe."

That vague response gave you some hope that you would get that toy, but in the end, you likely never received it.

Sales is no different.

If you hear anything but "yes," the answer is likely a "no"—and you should treat it as such. "Maybe" may not necessarily mean "no" forever, but at a minimum, it's a "no for now." So don't misinterpret the "maybe" response as a "yes."

If you hear a "maybe," slow yourself down and consider the following tips:

- **Don't respond right away.** Give yourself a minute to think about whether you can still turn this deal around.
- **Ask some follow-up questions.** Figure out why the person is reluctant to say "yes." Look at it from the other person's point of view.
- **Listen to learn** what else you might have to offer that could sweeten the deal enough to turn the "maybe" into a "yes."
- **Ask again.** Now that you have this new information, maybe the time is right to make your request a second time.
- **Don't insist.** If this "maybe" really is a firm "no," then pressuring the person into a "yes" is a bad idea. It will put the person and you in an awkward spot. And it could bruise your reputation and jeopardize future sales. I never pressure anyone into changing a "maybe" to a "yes" because it simply doesn't work.

Tough Lessons

A "no" is hard to hear, but that isn't the only tough lesson you'll learn along the way. Here are a few other truths I've learned the hard way:

1. Sometimes the answer is "no" because a "yes" will cost the other person money, trouble, or time.

Unless the person you are working with has a special relationship with you or owes you something, your request simply might not be reasonable for her. Thank her for her time and accept that this won't happen for both of you—right now.

2. If you ask the impossible, you can't expect a "yes," or at least a sincere "yes."

Just because you believe a vendor should be able to deliver what you need within the hour doesn't mean he can do it. The product might be located more than an hour away. He might have more than an hour's worth of commitments in line ahead of yours. His car might be in the shop.

Unreasonable expectations are a result of the growing sense of entitlement we all seem to be adopting because we are used to technology delivering what we want in an instant. But in the physical world, things can take a little longer.

Be patient, plan ahead, and do your research. Know before you ask whether what you're asking for is in any way, shape, or form possible.

3. You're going to feel guilty if you use your new superpower—the skill to sell—to get things you don't need from people who can't afford to give them.

I hear people all the time saying, "Just because you can doesn't mean you should."

I'm encouraging you to practice your new sales skills. I'm not encouraging you to take advantage of people. A lot of people—maybe even you—believe sales professionals take advantage of people. Maybe you've met unscrupulous salespeople who have lied to you, promised one thing but delivered another, or pitched such a hard sell that you agreed to spend more time, money, or energy than you have.

Those are not the kinds of sales tactics I'm encouraging at all.

To me, the sales process—official or unofficial—should be ethical, transparent, and honest and should leave you feeling like you gave as much as you got.

Don't take advantage of the kindness of people who would do anything for anybody—unless you really need their help. Instead, offer your help to them.

You will be rewarded with far more "yes" answers in the future if you build a reputation by selling ethically.

STEP FIVE IN ACTION

———— BE NICE ————

This book covers five important steps and many, many themes. And underlying them all is one single piece of advice that I believe will help you sell others on agreeing to whatever it is you want or need: Be nice.

When you're nice to people, they respond with trust, appreciation, and a "yes."

So why wouldn't you be nice?

When my husband and I moved to San Francisco, one of the things we missed most from back home was the food. We had constant cravings for our Southern comfort food: spicy fried chicken, fried okra, boiled peanuts, and cornbread. So we literally jumped for joy in the street when we discovered a Southern-style restaurant just a couple of miles from our house.

It's not in a great neighborhood, so we were afraid that it might not do well because of the location, but the owner has kept it alive. How? It's simple: He's nice.

My husband was the first to discover the place, and he ate lunch there. He talked it up when he got home, so we went together the following weekend.

When we walked in the door, the owner approached us. He recognized my husband and remembered where we were from. He recommended the fried chicken, which was out of this world, and he personally made sure we had enough hot sauce and sweet tea throughout our entire meal.

We didn't order dessert, but he brought it anyway: homemade buttermilk ice cream. I felt like I was at my grandma's house.

As soon as we got home, I posted a glowing review on Yelp. Five minutes later, I got a notification from Yelp that the owner had responded. He wrote how great it was to see my husband again and to meet me. He asked us to come back.

I have to say, he made me feel like I was down home. He made us customers for life with a single interaction. We go back all the time—and we're not the only ones. The place is in no danger of closing down, despite the sketchy block where it's located.

People like to go to the places where the staff is friendly, courteous, and helpful. People like to go to the places where they know everyone will be nice to them. Nice brings people back to you.

My friend has a sign hanging in her office that says, "In a world where you can be anything, be nice." I'm all for that, because being nice is a great sales tool—an effective sales tool.

No matter what else you have to sell, "nice" sells you. So make sure you're selling people the right thing.

No matter where you are or what you're doing, you're a representative of the place where you work. If you're nice at work but prickly everywhere else, that's a reflection on your company—and it will affect your ability to sell.

You are a walking advertisement for your organization and yourself at all times. If you bad-mouth your company when you're off the clock, you're selling the wrong thing. People like to repeat horror stories. Don't make the story about you or your employer.

If your nose is in your phone while people are trying to engage with you, you're selling them the wrong thing. You're selling them the idea that whomever you're texting or whatever app you're viewing is more important than the people standing right in front of you.

PRO TIP

Be present. As soon as someone tries to engage with you, give that person your full attention. Don't ask the person to wait for you while you finish a text or end a call. Be engaged immediately and throughout your entire interaction.

If you work your employees to the bone and then reward them at holiday time with a $10 gift card, you're selling the wrong thing. You're selling them something they might already think about you: that you're stingy and unappreciative.

It might be easier to snap at someone for messing up than it is to take a breath and ask the person why it happened. It might be easier to storm out of the room when you don't get your way than to say, "Thank you for your time," and shake hands before you go.

Easier isn't always what's best, but being nice definitely is.

Here are five ways to bake a little more "nice" into your personality:

1. Be approachable.

There's another place in my neighborhood where I really like to spend time after work. It's a hip restaurant that serves nice champagne and my favorite cheeses.

Still, when my husband and I moved to the East Coast, a considerable amount of time passed before we were able to return to the lounge. When we moved back to San Francisco and finally stopped by, the owner rolled out the red carpet for us. He said he missed us.

But that evening, a new bartender who wasn't working there when we left rubbed us the wrong way. "Sassy" does not even do enough to describe this kid. He was too cool for school. He acted like he was the prince and we were serfs. He acted like we didn't matter to him.

So once again, we stopped going—by choice this time.

We walk our dog, Biscuit, by the restaurant most evenings, though. One night, the owner came out and brought him some dog treats. Again, he said he missed us.

He also told us that business had been slow. He asked why we hadn't been in.

I told him. Almost 20 waiters, bartenders, chefs, and busboys work at the restaurant and lounge, and this one guy was ruining it for him.

Nobody had told him.

I'm an outgoing person, and I tend to make friends easily. So I used to chat with the owner all the time. His staff and other customers apparently don't.

Maybe that's because they find him unapproachable.

His business was suffering because one bartender was chasing people away, and nobody told the owner.

Be approachable. Coach your employees to be approachable. Your business could depend on it.

2. Show your personality.

My husband and I planned a night out with friends on New Year's Eve.

The day before, a cable technician had come over to fix whatever was wrong with our Wi-Fi. We had the cable connected, the router set up, and the TV mounted, but we couldn't get any signal.

So I had called the people at the cable company that afternoon, and they gave me a window for our service from 2 p.m. to 4 p.m. We had to leave for our double date at 5.

The tech called at 3:45 and said he was running late, that he'd be there as soon as he possibly could. I said OK, but I told him we had to leave the house at 5.

While he was on his way to our house, he called and asked me to describe the problem we were having. He asked a lot of questions, and he actually was able to diagnose the problem on the phone.

He arrived just before 4:30. I was all dressed up and ready to go out, but my husband had just walked in the door after work and had to get cleaned up. The cable guy had to be in the bedroom, where my husband usually gets ready.

You'd think he would have been in our way, but he made sure he wasn't. He apologized for being late and said he would be out in a hurry. He found the problem within a few minutes, explaining every step of the way what he was doing and what had happened.

As we waited for the router to boot up, he made small talk. He asked about our holiday plans. He told me about his.

He was friendly and funny. He seemed like someone we would like to make friends with.

Even though we were rushed and annoyed with the mistake the guy had made the day before, we felt happy that this tech was at our condo helping us. He was in and out of the bedroom in a matter of minutes. He acknowledged that we were in a hurry.

He finished up, but my husband wasn't ready yet, so he showed me a few tricks that our remote was programmed to do; those were new to me.

Once everything was finished, he thanked us and left. He left a card and asked us to answer an e-mail that would be coming our way, asking us what we thought of his service.

He was in our home for less than 20 minutes, but it was the most thorough encounter I have ever had with a technician, and among the most pleasant.

He read the situation and responded to it. He didn't make it worse by delaying us. He was personable and helpful.

He thanked us for being patient and wished us a happy new year.

The next day, I filled out the survey and gave him five stars.

He wasn't there to sell us anything, but he did. He sold us on changing our attitude about his company.

He's a walking advertisement for his company.

3. Do what you say you will.

A former colleague, Chase, just changed jobs. He was a researcher for a small nonprofit and wanted to try working at a big corporation.

His new boss was on the ball: Even the researchers at the corporation were supposed to try to sign their clients for additional work whenever possible. Chase came to me for advice because he knows that's the kind of consulting that I do.

A few months after he switched, I actually needed a researcher, so I gave Chase a call. I knew he would score a lot of points with his boss if he brought a new client to the firm.

Chase told me all about his services. He said he could do in-depth research for me and write a detailed report that would give me the market data I needed to make a big decision. It was so much fun to be working with my old colleague again.

I really liked his energy and his pitch. I hired him to do the research.

He charged me $4,500 and took four weeks to do the work. Then he e-mailed me his report, which was three pages.

It didn't tell me anything I didn't already know. It barely scratched the surface. It was a disappointment.

I let him know. After another week, he gave me another three pages, mostly graphics. Again, not enough.

I didn't hire him to do any more work after that.

I'm not sure if Chase talks bigger than he's able to deliver or if he just didn't put any effort into my job. But I had deliberately done him a favor by hiring him instead of my regular researcher.

And that was the second favor I had done for him.

The problem: He didn't deliver what he promised.

One of the best ways to say "thank you" to someone who has agreed to hire you, do you a favor, or say "yes" to a request is to do a good job in response.

It's important to do what you say you will do. Fall short of that, and the client or customer will never do business with you again.

4. Go out of your way.

Unexpected kindnesses are the most memorable.

I'll never forget the time an airline lost my suitcase after forcing me to check it, even though it was a carry-on bag. I wound up in St. John in the Virgin Islands without a bathing suit, a sundress, or my sandals.

For three days.

I had worn yoga pants on the plane, and they were a bit warm for Caribbean weather. Plus, they weren't appropriate to wear to nice restaurants. And I had worn them the entire day we traveled.

This was in the days before cell phones, and I wound up with a $75 bill for using the phone in my hotel to call the airline again and again. Still, no suitcase.

I was in tears by the time the airline operators had transferred me for the seventh time. But the seventh time was the charm.

The customer service rep told me she was sorry that I was dealing with this and that I had been passed around so much. She told me, "I'm going to find your bag."

None of the other six had said that. I believed her.

In the meantime, she said, go ahead and buy a bathing suit and a sundress, and she would make sure the airline reimbursed me.

She asked me for my phone number and said she would call and leave a message for me when she found my bag. That way, I could go to the beach instead of sitting in the hotel room making phone calls to check up on things.

An hour later, she called. My bag was in St. Croix, the next island over. Whoever wrote on the luggage tag had bad penmanship, and the bag had been misdelivered.

She couldn't deliver my bag that day because all the couriers were gone already. But she assured me it would be at my hotel in the morning. And it was.

This woman isn't in sales; she's in customer service. She solves problems, and she solved mine. I got my bag and was reimbursed for the bathing suit and sundress. And as a result, I wrote to the airline to compliment her because she actually took some responsibility to have a positive impact on someone who was having a really bad day—which she didn't have to do but did anyway.

That's what "nice" looks like.

5. Show your gratitude.

I always come back to this.

It bears repeating: Nobody does this life alone. Nobody is successful in a vacuum. Nobody is truly happy without people to help, befriend, and care about him or her. Surround yourself with the people you admire. Lean on them. Confide in them. Ask them for help.

And be grateful when they say "yes."

You don't have to send 100 Thanksgiving cards every year like I do. You just have to say "thank you" and mean it.

You just have to show your gratitude, whether you heard a "yes" or a "no."

Be grateful.

Review of the Five Steps

NOW THAT YOU KNOW my five-step process, start using it: Plan, look for opportunities, establish trust, ask for what you want, and follow up. And if you ever need a refresher, use this page as a quick and easy reference.

Step One: PLAN to sell. You're already selling every day—possibly without even knowing it. Now you can plan to sell on purpose.

Step Two: LOOK FOR OPPORTUNITIES to make unofficial sales. They're everywhere. They happen every day.

Step Three: ESTABLISH TRUST with the people you deal with when you ask for a sale, a favor, or help. Listen until you hear what the other person could get out of the transaction. Then you can give something and also get something.

Step Four: ASK FOR WHAT YOU WANT. Ask for the sale. You won't get anything unless you ask.

Step Five: FOLLOW UP with the people who help you. Even if you didn't get what you asked for, someone took the time to consider your request. Show your gratitude by keeping in touch, sending progress reports, and saying "thank you."

And, remember: Every job is a sales job—even yours.

EPILOGUE
Life Sales

EVERY JOB IS A sales job. And every day before, during, and after work, the selling continues.

You sell your children on doing their homework and brushing their teeth. You sell your husband on picking up the dry cleaning. You sell your book club on reading the novel you chose. You sell the waiter at your favorite restaurant on bringing you a salad instead of french fries.

Life is one sale after another.

Every day of your life, you try to talk someone into something, ask for a favor, or state your case with the hope of changing someone's mind.

These are sales—more specifically what I like to call "life sales."

You've been selling all your life, even though you're not a salesperson and probably don't want to be one.

By now, you know that every job, including yours, truly is a sales job in some way, shape, or form. And by now, you know that when you sell, there's no need to do it in a pushy, cheesy, or dishonest way.

And you know that my five-step process for a sale that benefits both you and the other person is a kind and effective way to negotiate with another person to get what you want, need, and deserve at work.

Well, that same process works when you're not at work.

You can use the skills you've learned by reading *Every Job Is a Sales Job* for a life sale, too.

The steps are the same, on the job or in your nonwork life:

1. Know what you want and make a plan to get it.

If you take the time to figure out exactly what you want and why it's important to you, you'll have a much easier time selling someone else on helping you get it. Coming up with a plan helps you sharpen your focus, set priorities, and prepare to explain your "ask" to another person. If you can't explain what you want, you're unlikely to get it.

2. Look for opportunities, and recognize them when you see them.

Opportunities for unofficial sales are all around you. The same is true for life sales—once you start paying attention. Once you start looking, you'll see the opportunity to request things that might make your day easier, solve a problem, or get you anything from a deal on concert tickets to a warning instead of a ticket when you get pulled over. You'll see how many of your daily interactions can become life sales.

3. Establish trust with the people you ask to help you or do stuff for you.

Listen; observe; be nice. Learn enough about the person you're dealing with to know what you can do for him or her in exchange for the favor you need. Lots of people will do nice things for you just because you're nice to them. A life sale, like an unofficial sale at work, is something you come by honestly. It's something that helps the other person, too. It's something you get because you're willing to give.

4. Ask for what you want.

It's OK to ask others to help, even if what you want might not seem important to anyone but you. It's OK to ask the barista at the coffee shop to remake your drink if he got it wrong the first time. It's OK to request the afternoon off so you can see your kid perform in a school play. It's OK to give yourself permission not only to ask for what you want, but to get it.

5. Follow up and be grateful.

Whether you hear a "yes" or a "no" when you try to make a life sale, someone has taken the time to listen to and consider your request, so say "thank you." Every time you make a life sale, you create the opportunity to make another one sometime in the future. Keep in touch with the people who help you. You never know when you can repay the favor—or when you might have another favor to ask of the same person.

———————   ———————

These five steps combine into a sustainable process that will help you see the opportunities that are literally right in front of you—opportunities to get what you need, want, and deserve every day.

This process will help you confidently ask for what you want, need, and deserve. It will prepare you to respond in just the right way, whether you hear a "yes" or a "no." And it will help you build lifelong relationships with people who have already proved that they are happy to help you.

Whether you're negotiating with a car salesperson for a better deal or an ex to trade weekends with the kids, this is the process that will help you get what you need and want. This is a proven formula to use when you ask someone to pick up your child from school if you can't. It applies when you try to use a coupon that expired yesterday to buy something today. Try it out next time you need your dentist to squeeze you in for an unscheduled visit.

At work and at home, we spend every day in sales mode. Every interaction is a transaction. Every request, compromise, and tug-of-war you engage in every day requires you to sell something to another person: a viewpoint, an idea, or an action. If you don't sell it, you won't hear a "yes."

Now that you know how to sell, sell more.
Sell at work and at home.
It works for me. It can work for anyone.
It can work for you. It already does.

Dear Reader –

I want to thank you so very much for reading Every Job Is a Sales Job!

If you picked up this book thinking you were not a salesperson and wanted nothing to do with sales, I hope I've changed your mind. I hope the stories and tips in the book have helped you to discover and embrace your inner salesperson.

I appreciate you buying the book and spending your time reading it. I hope you'll share your future sales successes with me at www.drcindy.com

– Dr. Cindy

Index

About the Author

DR. CINDY McGOVERN is known as the "First Lady of Sales."
She speaks and consults internationally on sales, interper-
sonal communication, and leadership. Dr. Cindy holds a
doctorate in organizational communication and worked as
a professor of communication before starting Orange Leaf
Consulting, a sales management and consulting firm in
San Francisco. She has helped hundreds of companies and
individuals create dramatic and sustainable growth. Dr.
Cindy regularly coaches both professional sales employees
and those whose jobs are not sales-related in an effort to
help them both take advantage of opportunities to bring
more business to their companies. For more information:
www.drcindy.com.